WHY VOTE LEAVE

Daniel Hannan has been Conservative MEP for South East England since 1999. He writes frequently for the *Daily Telegraph*, *Daily Mail*, *Guardian*, *CapX*, and *Washington Examiner*. He is the author of the award-winning *How We Invented Freedom & Why It Matters*.

WHY VOTE LEAVE

Daniel Hannan

HEAD
of ZEUS

First published in the UK in 2016 by Head of Zeus, Ltd

9 7 5 3   4 6 8

A catalogue record for this book is available from
the British Library.

ISBN (HB): 9781784977108
ISBN (E): 9781784977092

Typeset by Adrian McLaughlin

Printed in the UK by Clays Ltd, St Ives Plc

Head of Zeus Ltd
Clerkenwell House
45–47 Clerkenwell Green
London ECIR OHT

WWW.HEADOFZEUS.COM

CONTENTS

FIGURES

INTRODUCTION

PLEASE SACK ME

I STILL REMEMBER my utter, nerveless shock. It was my first day in Brussels as a Member of the European Parliament (MEP) and, having found my office and done the basic tour, I was invited to hand in my plane ticket for reimbursement.

When I saw the sum that I was being given, I assumed that there had been some mistake. 'No, no,' I told the helpful lady, 'I've just come from Heathrow.'

'No mistake, Monsieur,' she replied brightly. 'That's the kilometrage rate from London.'

'But it can't be. I mean, there's no way anyone could spend that sum travelling here from London.'

'That's right, Monsieur, that's how the rate is

calculated.' She went on to explain that when MEPs travel from their constituencies to one of the two parliamentary locations (the European Parliament meets, at vast expense, in both Brussels and Strasbourg), they are reimbursed on the basis of the priciest notional fare, plus an extra 'time and distance allowance'. Even if you really did travel at the top business class fare, you would make a tidy sum. But if you were prepared to fly EasyJet, you could trouser the better part of £800 pounds a week – tax-free, because it counted as expenses rather than income.

The next desk belonged to the 'general expenses' official. He explained that we were entitled to nearly £3,500 a month as a bloc grant.

'What, you mean to rent an office with?'

'No, no, we give you offices in Brussels and in Strasbourg.'

'For computers and equipment, then?'

'No, you get that, too. It's for other incidental expenses like postage and petrol.'

'Seriously? Three-and-a-half grand a month?'

'As I say, sir, it's an unconditional grant. You don't have to submit receipts. You just nominate which bank account it goes into.'

After him was the staff adviser. It turned out that we would get more than €12,000 a month to hire people.

Which is, if you think about it, more than enough to take on a secretary, a researcher and a press officer, and still have a large dollop left over for your wife.

I wish I could say that the practice of hiring immediate family members was beneath British representatives, but the reality is that people respond to incentives regardless of nationality. If the kitchen is dirty enough, bacteria will breed, whether in Palermo or Pinner. If anything, the Brits were unusually keen on keeping things within the family. As a senior French MEP once put it to me: 'What is it about you English? You employ your wives and you sleep with your staff!'

Why am I telling you about my first day at work? For two reasons.

First, to draw your attention to the gap between theory and practice. Because the European Union (EU) was launched from exalted motives – peace and co-operation among nations – there can be a temptation to give it the benefit of the doubt. We often half-pretend that we are dealing with some fantasy EU, one that rises above the grubbiness of politics and embodies a lofty ideal. It seems almost bad taste to look in too much detail at the one which has, in fact, taken shape before us with its dodgy accounts and its private jets.

The way in which MEPs are remunerated is one small example of how, rather than being pure, the EU is often, in the exact sense, corrupting – that is, it makes otherwise good people behave in bad ways. I know several MEPs who came to Brussels without feeling especially strongly about closer integration, but who drank in federalist assumptions as they guzzled down their allowances.

What is true of the MEPs is equally true, as we shall see, of the many giant corporations, mega-charities, think-tanks, non-governmental organizations (NGOs), professional associations and lobbyists who have learned how to make a living out of the Brussels system. These groups are, as you might expect, the Praetorian Guard of the 'Remain' campaign. For their executives, it's not about sovereignty or democracy; it's about mortgages and school fees.

But I have another motive for telling you about MEPs' expenses. I want you to understand why I am now, in effect, inviting you to serve me with my P45.

What will change when Britain leaves the EU? Less, certainly, than some campaigners will claim. There will be some democratic gains and some financial gains; and there will also, I hope, be a psychological gain, by which I mean that we'll have a renewed sense of national purpose and optimism. But, on a technical level – certainly when it comes to trade – most existing structures will almost certainly be left in place.

As the leader of Britain Stronger in Europe (BSE), the former Marks and Spencer boss, Lord Rose, honestly admitted at the launch of the 'Remain' campaign, before horrified spin-doctors could shut him up:

> Nothing is going to happen if we come out of Europe in the first five years, probably. There will be absolutely no change. Then, if you look back ten years later, there will have been some change, and if you look back fifteen years later there will have been some.

Indeed. The main effect of leaving the EU will be that Britain begins to follow a different trajectory, less dependent on an enervated and declining eurozone and more focused on the rest of the world. No jobs will be lost – except those of a few hundred British Eurocrats and MEPs, including me.

So what makes me volunteer to be one of the few redundancies? Why do I aim to abolish my well-remunerated and comfortable position? Why am I asking you to fire me?

Believe me, it's not out of any anti-European senti-ment. I speak French and Spanish, and have lived and worked all over the Continent. I know of almost no one who objects to the idea of neighbouring countries coming together for mutual gain, arbitrating their disputes peacefully and seeking to tackle cross-border problems jointly. If the EU were about international collaboration rather than supranational coercion, no one would have a problem with it.

Equally, if being a good European means believing in the things that have elevated and ennobled European civilization – the rule of law, parliamentary democracy, personal liberty – then sign me up. My quarrel with the EU has to do with its abandonment of these ideals. Instead of the rule of law, we have the imperative of political union: when the dots and commas of the treaties stand in the way of deeper integration, they are unhesitatingly set aside. Instead of parliamentary democracy, we're governed by unelected officials who reach their decisions in secret, often after being lobbied by vested interests. Instead of personal liberty, we have a mass of pettifogging regulation that makes us poorer as well as less free.

If the EU were simply about trade and summits, there'd never have been any controversy, and we wouldn't now be holding a referendum. The trouble is that, in its determination to jam its nations together, it recognizes no distinction between cross-border and domestic spheres. Again and again, it has pursued regulation as an end in itself – not in response to an identified need, but as a step towards federation.

Almost no aspect of national life is untouched by Brussels rules. In the very week that David Cameron began his campaign to persuade Britain to remain in the EU, his ministers were admitting that they couldn't cut the 5 per cent VAT on sanitary products because it was against EU regulations. At the same time, as if to taunt his powerlessness, MEPs voted to overturn Britain's requirement that Internet companies provide filters so that parents of young children can screen out obscene sites.

Now there are arguments for and against porn filters. (I can see fewer arguments for taxing tampons, which are surely not a luxury item.) But never mind which side you are on: issues of this sort surely ought to be decided by our own elected representatives, whom we can then re-elect or otherwise on the basis of their records.

How did the question of Internet pornography become an EU issue? Aspects of it might conceivably be global but it is hard to see any European angle. And how is it that Britain, the Mother of Parliaments, cannot lift a tax on sanitary products?

Why, by the same token, should it be up to Brussels

to ban traditional light bulbs and oblige us to have the dimmer sort – many of which have to be imported from China, at great cost to the environment?

Why should it be up to Brussels to ban high-power vacuum cleaners, hair-driers, toasters and other electrical appliances? As my wife remarked at the time: 'Never mind keeping the state out of the bedroom: can't you keep it out of our bloody kitchen?'

It's not that the EU is necessarily wrong about all these things. But how did we reach the stage where such issues are decided by a Continent-wide bureaucracy and then handed down uniformly to 600 million people?

Again and again, matters where you would think there was no European angle turn out to be within the jurisdiction of Brussels. For example, one of David Cameron's first initiatives as prime minister was to use the uncollected money in forgotten bank accounts to fund charitable initiatives. He had to drop the idea when he was told that it would conflict with EU law.

I am required to drive my children around in booster seats until they reach either a minimum height or twelve years of age. I had looked forward to discarding the wretched yoghurt-encrusted blobs much sooner (the car-seats, I mean, not the children). Whether or not you agree with me, how is this an issue that needs to be imposed rigidly across twenty-eight nations?

The list goes on and on. The hassle of opening a bank account, with all your old utilities bills? That's the EU's Money Laundering Directive. The end of weekly recycling collections? That's the Landfill Directive. The ban on minimum alcohol pricing? That's the Technical Standards Directive.

These laws are not agreements among states. They are the legislative acts of an entity that itself aspires to statehood.

The EU question comes down, in the end, to legal supremacy. Who, ultimately, runs Britain? Can we make our own laws, or must we recognize EU primacy? Are we an independent country, co-operating with our neighbours, or a sub-unit within a larger European polity?

Legal supremacy is what distinguishes the EU from every other international association. The European Treaties do not simply bind the twenty-eight members as states; they create a new legal order, with precedence over national laws, directly binding upon individuals and businesses within each country.

The EU's legal primacy is not restricted to cross-border issues. It arguably makes sense to agree common standards for international economic activity, just as it makes sense to have common rules for international dial codes, bank transfers and so on. But EU rules, unlike those in other trade associations, don't stop at national borders. They fall on all citizens and all firms, including small enterprises that do no export business.

How many British businesses trade with the EU? The proportion is slighter than most people realize. If you bought this book in the United Kingdom, you were contributing to our domestic GDP but not to our international trade. If you stopped for a cup of coffee afterwards, or bought a newspaper, or had your hair cut, you were likewise adding to our national turnover, not to our overseas commerce. Fully 79 per cent of business activity in the United Kingdom is in this category: wholly internal. Most firms, indeed, trade only within a ten-mile radius of where they are sited. Of the 21 per cent of our GDP that depends on overseas commerce, 10 per cent is accounted for by trade with the EU, and 11 per cent by trade with the rest of the world.[1]

In other words, for the sake of the 10 per cent of our economy that is linked to the EU, we must apply 100 per cent of EU rules to 100 per cent of our businesses. And, as we shall see, even that 10 per cent figure will soon be out of date. Our trade with the EU is in deficit

1 House of Commons Foreign Affairs Select Committee, 3 November 2015

and falling, while our trade with the rest of the world is in surplus and rising.

I make this observation in no triumphant spirit. I write as someone who loves Europe. I am Francophile, Germanophile, Hispanophile, Hellenophile, Italophile, Lusophile – but I'm not Europhile, at least not if being Europhile means wanting to remain part of an essentially undemocratic, remote and self-serving Brussels system.

The promises on which the EU was built have proved false. European integration was supposed to make people wealthier; but the EU has fallen further and further behind in relative terms, from 30 per cent of the world economy in 1980 to 17 per cent today.[2] It was supposed to make participating nations get on better, but the euro and migration crises have served to stoke rather than soothe national antagonisms.

Indeed, the euro and Schengen alone should serve to discredit the European project. It's not just that the authors of those schemes are sticking mulishly to them as though nothing had changed. It's that they want to extend the same flawed logic to other areas, seeing deeper integration as the solution rather than the problem. Or, to be more precise, seeing deeper integration as an objective that justifies any number of problems.

2   IMF, *World Economic Outlook*

The euro must be maintained, regardless of the cost in higher unemployment and lost growth. Schengen, too, must be upheld, regardless of the impact on security or, come to that, refugee welfare. Whatever the question, the answer is always 'more Europe'.

Does that have to be the answer for Britain, too? Having tried and failed to convince our friends to go in a different direction, must we submit ourselves to their project?

Surely we can do better. We can trade and co-operate with our allies on the Continent while living under our own laws. We can remain sympathetically involved with the affairs of our immediate neighbours while also giving due weight to our older alliances. We can adapt to the global realities of the digital age.

This referendum is our chance. We can see the direction in which the EU is going, and we know now that no renegotiation can alter it from within. As Europe shrivels economically, we have a one-off opportunity to stand amicably aside and negotiate a better relationship, based on free trade and self-government.

Seize that opportunity and, as well as recovering our democracy, we might jolt the EU out of its disastrous introversion. If we cannot lead by persuasion, let us lead by example.

1

WHO WOULD JOIN
THE EU TODAY?

ASK YOURSELF SOMETHING. If the United Kingdom were not already a member of the European Union, would you vote to join?

It is never easy to answer hypothetical questions, of course; but it's worth noting how people feel in the Western European countries that stayed out. Perhaps the non-EU nations most comparable to Britain, being neither ex-communist nor microstates, are Iceland, Norway and Switzerland. In all of them, there are solid and settled majorities against joining the EU.

In Iceland, which formally withdrew its application for membership in 2015, voters oppose joining by

50.1 per cent to 34.2 per cent.[3] In Norway, the feeling is even more emphatic: 72.0 per cent to 18.1 per cent, a balance that has changed little in over a decade.[4] In Switzerland, opinion polls on the EU are rarer, because membership was widely seen to have been killed off when a referendum in 2001 resulted in a massive 76.8 per cent against reopening accession talks. Still, for what it's worth, the latest survey shows that 82.0 per cent of Swiss citizens support their current bilateral arrangements.[5]

None of these countries has a perfect deal with the EU, because perfection is unattainable, at least in the field of international relations. But, whatever minor annoyances they have, they prefer their present freedoms to stepping on to a conveyor belt whose far end they can't see. Supporters of membership have never been able to answer the question raised by the Centre Party's Anne Enger Lahnstein, who led the successful 'No' campaign when Norway held its accession referendum in 1994: 'To what problem is the EU a solution?'

Back in 1975, when the United Kingdom held her previous referendum on membership, that question

3   *Morgunbladið*, 17 August 2015
4   *Nationen*, 29 December 2015
5   *Sicherheit 2015*, ETH Zürich

seemed to have an answer. The European Economic Community (EEC) was supposed to be all about free trade. Most British people can no longer remember the mid-1970s, but those years were arguably our lowest moment as a nation. It was the era of the three-day week, government controls on prices and incomes, power cuts, double-digit inflation, deficits and constant strikes. There was an almost universal view, certainly among pundits and politicians, that Britain was in irrevocable decline.

Throughout the 1960s and 1970s, the UK had been outperformed by every European economy. 'Britain is a tragedy – it has sunk to borrowing, begging, stealing until North Sea oil comes in,' said Henry Kissinger. The *Wall Street Journal* in 1975, the year of the referendum, was even blunter: 'Goodbye, Great Britain: it was nice knowing you.'

When British people looked across the Channel, they saw what looked like a success story. The then six members of the EEC had suffered far more damage during the Second World War than Britain had. Their factories had been bombed, their bridges thrown down. And yet, they had somehow bounced back – indeed, not just bounced back, but comprehensively outperformed Britain and the Commonwealth.

In retrospect, we can see why the UK lagged behind.

She had emptied her treasury and amassed an unprecedented debt in order to defeat Hitler. By 1945, Britain had borrowed £21 billion, an incredible sum in that era, much of it from the United States. Unlike in the European states that were deemed to have started afresh after the overthrow of fascism, this debt was not remitted. The repayments were a drag on growth for the next thirty years – indeed, the very last instalment on one American loan was made only in 2006. As well as the immediate budgetary cost, successive governments sought to inflate the debt away, which had a knock-on effect on productivity and competitiveness. By the 1970s, Britain was close to collapse. Small wonder that sensible people looked enviously at the model of 'Rhineland capitalism' that had apparently been responsible for Western Europe's *Wirtschaftswunder* or 'economic miracle'.

In fact, although no one knew it at the time, the *Wirtschaftswunder* was coming to an end just as Britain joined. The post-war years had been very good for Continental Europe. Although the war had indeed wrecked much infrastructure, an educated and industrious workforce remained in place to rebuild it. The boom was fuelled by unprecedented migration from the countryside to industrial centres and from the Mediterranean to northern coalfields.

Western Europe, moreover, profited from massive external assistance. America's Marshall Aid programme disbursed an extraordinary $13 billion, on top of the $12 billion separately contributed by the US between 1948 and 1952. Arguably even more valuable was the US defence guarantee, which allowed European governments to divert military spending to civil projects.

By the 1970s, though, the sugar-rush was wearing off. We can now see that the 1974 oil shock was the beginning of a relative decline for Western Europe that has lasted to the present day. Britain's timing could not have been worse. She joined just as the growth-spurt was ending in Europe, and starting in the rest of the world.

The combined economies of the present twenty-eight members have shrunk, according to the International Monetary Fund (IMF), from 36 per cent of world GDP in 1973, when Britain joined, to 17 per cent in 2015 – and that decline is accelerating. If we count only the fifteen states that were in the EU before the ex-communist countries joined in 2004, the relative contraction is even sharper.

Let's ask the question again. If Britain were not already in the EU, would anyone seriously be proposing that we join?

Back in the 1950s, regional trade blocs looked like the future. Freight costs were high, refrigeration expensive, and exporters tended to look to their nearest neighbours.

Even then, Britain was something of an exception. A far more open and trading economy than any of the six original EEC members, she had long been in the habit of importing food and commodities from more distant continents. As Charles de Gaulle put it in 1963, when explaining his decision to veto Britain's entry:

> The question is whether Great Britain can now place herself, like the Continent and with it, inside a genuinely common tariff, renounce all Commonwealth preferences, cease any pretence that her agriculture be privileged, and, more than that, treat her engagements with the other countries of the free trade area as null and void.

Although many British politicians, at the time and afterwards, resented what they saw as an act of ingratitude from a man Britain had succoured during the war, the old general arguably had a keener appreciation of Britain's global vocation than had his British counterpart, Harold Macmillan. His analysis of Britain's economic profile, at any rate, is hard to dispute:

England in effect is insular, she is maritime, she is linked through her interactions, her markets and her supply lines to the most diverse and often the most distant countries; she pursues essentially industrial and commercial activities, and only slight agricultural ones. She has, in all her doings, very marked and very original habits and traditions.

True, and very sensible habits and traditions they were. After all, the purpose of trade is to swap on the back of differences – to purchase from overseas what you cannot produce yourself without disproportionate cost. The most successful markets are therefore precisely, to quote de Gaulle, 'the most diverse'.

We can argue about whether it ever made sense for Britain to abandon a truly pluralist global trading system – one which brought together agrarian, commodity-based, industrial and service-oriented economies – for a cluster of similar advanced economies at the Western tip of the Eurasian landmass. But, whether or not it made sense at the time, it plainly makes no sense today.

Never before has geographical proximity mattered less. In the Internet age, a company in Luton can as easily do business with a firm in Ludhiana, India, as with one in Ljubljana, Slovenia. Indeed, more easily.

The Indian company, unlike the Slovenian one, will be English-speaking. It will share the British company's accountancy methods and unwritten business etiquette. If there is a dispute between the two parties, it will be arbitrated according to common-law norms with which both are familiar.

When it comes to investment, the natural affinities between the UK and India – affinities of kinship and migration as well as of law and language – are palpable. Britain is the third-largest investor in India, and many of the British firms that operate there, such as JCB, see no point in being in the EU. India, for its part, is the third-largest investor in the UK, owning more here than in the other twenty-seven members of the EU combined.

When it comes to trade, though, it is a very different story. JCB cannot sell its machinery tariff-free from India to the UK, any more than can Tata from the UK to India. Why? Because commerce is controlled by the European Commission. When Britain joined the EEC in 1973, she surrendered to Brussels the right to sign independent trade agreements. The Common External Tariff was imposed in stages, artificially redirecting Britain's trade from global to European markets – and in the process, wrecking the ports of Glasgow and Liverpool which found themselves on the wrong side of the country.

As long as she remains in the EU, Britain has no vote and no voice in the World Trade Organization. She is instead represented there by one twenty-eighth of a European Commissioner – at present, as it happens, a former sociology lecturer from Sweden.

Although supporters of the EU like to talk of Britain being present at the top tables, the real top tables these days are global rather than regional. Most standards – whether on food additives, vehicle safety or bank deposits – are determined internationally. Other countries are independently represented in the bodies that set them. But while Switzerland, New Zealand, Canada and so on have one voice each, the EU states reach a common position beforehand and are represented, more often than not, by the relevant European Commission officials. Britain is thus often obliged to pursue a more illiberal position than her interests dictate.

Trade is a good example. The Common Commercial Policy drags the UK into a more protectionist trade policy than she would have chosen for herself. The EU's common position must give due weight to the interests of various vested interests around Europe: Italian textile workers, Polish farmers, French film-makers. France, for example, made it a precondition of trade talks with the United States that the audio-visual sector be excluded – a massive exclusion when we consider that, on some measures, Hollywood is the second-largest overseas revenue earner for the US.

Of all the twenty-eight EU states, Britain is by far the hardest hit by the Common Commercial Policy. Twenty-six of the other twenty-seven members sell the majority of their exports to the rest of the EU. Britain and Greece are the only two EU nations that trade more overseas than in Europe and, in Britain's case, the gap is starting to widen seriously.

In addition, as Figure One shows, the EU has been especially slow to negotiate trade deals with Britain's major trade partners. Of Britain's top ten non-EU markets, Brussels has trade agreements in place with only two – Switzerland and South Korea.

Of course, having no trade agreement doesn't mean having no trade. It means, rather, that trade is restricted, subject to various forms of tariff and non-tariff barriers. Despite these barriers, though, British trade with non-EU states is in surplus and growing, while her trade with the EU is in deficit and shrinking.

Figure Two, sourced from HM Treasury Pink Books stretching back to 1958, shows how the balance between UK exports to the EU and exports to the rest of the world is changing. It's true, of course, that developing countries are bound to grow faster than

Fig. 1

ANTI-BRITISH
TARIFFS

Trading partner	Value of exports (£m)	Status	Length of negotiations
United States	37,350	FTA (TTIP) under negotiation	Since July 2013
China	14,075	Stand-alone investment under negotiation	Since November 2013
Switzerland	10,398	FTA in place	December 1994–June 1999
Hong Kong	6,354	no negotiations underway	N/A
United Arab Emirates	6,057	Negotiations frozen in 2008 by the GCC* due to the EU's insistence on political demands	Since 1990
South Korea	5,628	FTA in place	May 2007–October 2010
India	4,822	Negotiations frozen	Since June 2007
Japan	4,272	FTA under negotiation	Since April 2013
Russia	4,142	No negotiations underway – both sides have imposed sanctions	N/A
Saudi Arabia	3,891	Negotiations frozen in 2008 by the GCC* due to the EU's insistence on political demands	Since 1990

* The Gulf Cooperation Council: Bahrain, Kuwait, Oman, Qatar, Saudi Arabia and the United Arab Emirates.

Sources: ONS, European Commission, Open Europe Research

Fig. 2

DECLINING
EU

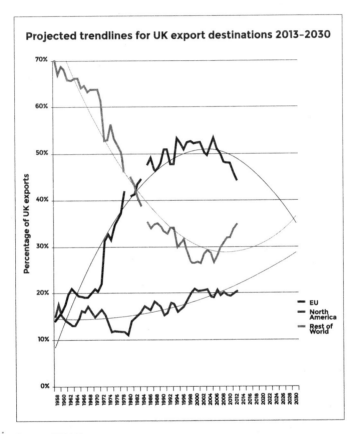

Projected trendlines for UK export destinations 2013–2030

Source: HM Treasury

developed ones, but this alone does not explain the EU's decline. To illustrate that point, the United States and Canada – hardly developing countries – have been shown separately from the EU and the rest of the world.

The figures eloquently tell the story of Britain's relationship with her immediate neighbours. In the 1970s, as the Common External Tariff was imposed, there was a massive shift from global to European markets. This shift did not take place organically but as a direct result of the new levies and duties imposed by Brussels. It continued throughout the 1980s and into the early 1990s before levelling off. Then, as the debt crisis began, it went into sharp decline.

It's true that the debt crisis won't last for ever. But there is no reason to suppose that the EU will recover its share of the world economy. All the long-term trends are against it, not least demography: with the exceptions of Scandinavia and the British Isles, Europe faces a massive population decline and, as the population declines, the ratio of workers to pensioners will fall.

In any case, it won't do to continue to blame the eurozone's continuing underperformance on the 2008 debt crisis. Every other region of the world has recovered but, incredibly, the eurozone's economy was no larger in 2015 than in 2008. According to the IMF, 2016 will see Canada grow by 2.3 per cent, the US

by 2.8 per cent, China by 6.3 per cent and India by
7.5 per cent. The UK will grow by 2.1 per cent, and
the other non-euro European states by 3.0 per cent.
But the eurozone, after eight years of stagnation, is
expected to manage only 1.6 per cent growth.

Plainly there is a structural problem that goes well
beyond the weaknesses exposed by the banking crisis.
And it is clear enough what that structural problem is.
It is the euro itself. The reason that the debt crisis was so
much more serious in the eurozone than anywhere else is
that monetary union forced a number of states to pursue
policies that exacerbated their economic woes. During
the boom years, to the alarm of observers, the peripheral
eurozone states were obliged to cut interest rates at a
time when every orthodox economist of Left or Right
would have decreed a rate rise to prevent a bubble.

Then, when the crash came, these same states were
unable to cushion the blow with a temporary devalu-
ation, and so had to raise taxes during the downturn.

Nor, incidentally, should we assume that the euro
crisis is over. The members of the monetary union
remain cyclically and structurally misaligned. Several
analysts fear that France or Italy or both will experience a Greek-style meltdown.

Be that as it may, the leaders of the EU have
plainly made their choice. For years, perhaps decades,

to come, they will concentrate on keeping the single currency intact at all costs while the rest of the world surges ahead.

Does Britain, despite her global links, want to remain attached to such a stagnant and unambitious customs union? Just how low does her trade with the EU need to fall before global commercial freedom is seen to matter more than a minority say in the setting of Brussels regulations?

As we can see from Figure Two, one of the favourite claims of British 'Remain' campaigners is false. Supporters of the EU like to tell anyone who'll listen that 'around half our exports' go to the EU. Of course, 'around' is a flexible word. In 2006, 54.7 per cent of Britain's exports went to the EU. In 2015, it was 44.6 per cent. Where will it be ten years from now? Where twenty years from now? At what point will we drop the bizarre argument that, for the sake of a dwindling minority of our commerce, we must merge our political institutions with those of some other countries? Will our children look back at the 2016 referendum and wonder why we missed such a unique opportunity to step amicably off the bus?

The question with which I opened the chapter answers itself. Had Britain, at the outset, negotiated a relationship with the EEC based on free trade rather than full membership, almost no one would now be pushing to join.

That, of course, is not quite the same as saying that we should leave. Lots of things that we wouldn't invent today survive through custom, familiarity and change-aversion. The QWERTY keyboard was designed in the 1870s to space out letters that were frequently used together, and so prevent jams at the ribbon. Now that keyboards are electronic, it would make more sense to lay the letters out in alphabetical order – making typing both easier to learn and quicker to perform. What keeps QWERTY in business? Inertia. Too many of us are used to the existing keyboards and can't easily retrain our fingers. As the great eighteenth-century philosopher and MP Edmund Burke used to argue, it is not enough to show that you are proposing something better; it must be better by a sufficient margin to justify the upheaval of getting there.

Is the EU like a QWERTY keyboard? Does the hassle of change – of putting new regulatory struc-tures in place and negotiating new trade deals – outweigh the advantages of bringing back freedom and independence?

No, for four reasons. First, because the EU, unlike a keyboard, is constantly changing. Choosing to stay in is not the same as choosing to stay put; rather, it is choosing to remain on a conveyor-belt. Second, because, as I have tried to show in this chapter, the world, too, is changing. The assumption that under-pinned the UK's accession in the 1970s has been falsified: instead of joining a vibrant and growing free trade area, we have shackled ourselves to the only trade bloc on the planet that is experiencing no significant growth. Third, because the costs of staying in, in sovereignty and economic freedom, as well as in straightforward budget contributions, are rising, while globalization has cut the cost of leaving. Fourth, because the inertia that has held us in the EU is not just emotional; it is also institutional. We fear change, not only because risk-aversion is in our genes, but also because the vested interests that have grown up around the status quo keep telling us that change would be disastrous. And perhaps it would be – for them.

2

THE TYRANNY OF
THE STATUS QUO

WILL THE EU firehose money at the 'Remain' campaign? Bizarre as it sounds, Brussels institutions have an opt-out from the spending caps that apply to the British organizations on either side.

Rules on how to conduct a UK referendum were laid down for the first time in the Political Parties, Elections and Referendums Act (2000), brought in following a political donations scandal. Tony Blair seems originally to have wanted legislation that applied only to general elections but when the Neill Commission, on which the legislation was based, recommended including referendums within the same system, he could hardly refuse. He was, however, determined to exempt EU institutions because he was still, at that time, hoping to hold a referendum on joining the euro. So the statutory limits apply to spending by political parties and other bodies, but not to the EU.

Should we, then, expect a torrent of EU-funded 'information'? Similar things have happened in other member states during referendums, and the Commission has reserved its right to intervene directly. In a reply to a written parliamentary question in January 2016, it stated: 'The European Commission carries out the tasks conferred upon it by the Treaties, which include promoting the general interest of the Union and taking appropriate initiatives to that end. The provision of factual information about the EU is part of this task.'

Still, it seems unlikely that Eurocrats will be so tactically inept as to blunder in themselves. Their frank talk about the need for a federal Europe riles British voters, and they know it. More to the point, they don't need to intervene directly. It makes far more sense for them to act through third parties.

Instead of spending money on Brussels-branded propaganda, which would be likely to do more harm than good, the EU will continue to fund proxies in the UK to make the 'Remain' argument on its behalf. These proxies include local government bodies, universities, charities, think-tanks, trade associations and other non-state actors.

It makes sense as a strategy. When we hear Eurocrats arguing (to pluck an example from the air) that the EU helps preserve endangered habitats, our first reaction is: 'Well, they would say that, wouldn't they?' But when we hear precisely the same argument from environmental lobby groups, it sounds disinterested. We almost never hear an interviewer ask whether the lobby groups are in receipt of EU grants, and we wouldn't think to investigate for ourselves.

Sure enough, on 26 January 2016, a letter appeared in the *Independent* signed by the heads of various green pressure groups. It was signed, too, by the immediate past chairmen of some environmental quangos, because serving chairmen by convention don't sign letters of this sort. It warned against a British exit ('Brexit') on grounds that EU laws had 'a hugely positive effect' on the environment. It did not attempt to explain why a post-EU Britain wouldn't simply retain or replicate – or even improve – these 'hugely positive' laws. As so often, there was a mildly insulting implication that voters needed to have such things handed down by their betters. What was really interesting, though, was the signatures at the end, representing universities, Natural England, the Green Alliance, the RSPB, the Natural Environment Research Council and so on. Of the twelve organizations named, the European Commission funds eight directly. Of course, 'protect our countryside' sounds so much prettier than 'protect our grants'.

Between now and polling day, we can expect to be bombarded by many more statements from NGOs saying that, although they have no formal position on EU membership as such, they feel it only right to state that, from the narrow perspective of their particular field of activity, the balance is in favour of membership.

How can we be so sure that this will be the 'Remain' side's tactic? Because we have seen it used before. It has been employed in other member states holding referendums on European issues. And it has been employed in the United Kingdom.

The last time that Britain had to approve a major transfer of power to Brussels was in 2007, when she ratified the Lisbon Treaty. That treaty had begun life as the European Constitution, and several EU states, including Britain, had promised to put it to a referendum. When France and the Netherlands voted 'No' in 2005, the document was renamed the 'Lisbon Treaty' and put through without referendums (except in Ireland, which voted 'No' and was made to vote again).

Labour ministers felt vulnerable to the accusation that they had weaselled out of their referendum promise, and wanted to try to make the Lisbon Treaty more palatable. How did they do it? By invoking supposedly neutral third-party endorsements. When he introduced the bill to ratify Lisbon in 2007, the then foreign secretary, David Miliband, made a great song and dance about the fact that it wasn't just Labour Europhiles who backed the text. A whole range of NGOs, he told the House of Commons, had also come out in favour.

'The NSPCC has pledged its support, as have One World Action, ActionAid and Oxfam,' he said, looking pleased with himself. 'Environmental organizations support the treaty provisions on sustainable development and even the commission of bishops supports the treaty. This is a coalition, not of ideology, but integrity.'

Integrity? A few moments on Google (which, incidentally, spent around seven million euros lobbying the EU last year) revealed that every organization the foreign secretary had cited was in receipt of EU subventions. Most of them, it turned out, had also received grants from the British government. Hardly surprising, then, that they should dutifully endorse a treaty supported by their paymasters.

What was surprising was the extent of their financial dependency. When Mr Miliband sat down, I fired off a written question asking the European Commission how much money it had paid these organizations. It turned out that, in the previous year, ActionAid, the NSPCC, One World Action and Oxfam had between them been given €43,051,542.95.

Just think about that sum for a moment. Can organizations in receipt of such colossal subsidies legitimately call themselves 'non-governmental'? Can they claim to be independent? Can they even describe themselves as charities – at least in the sense that we commonly understand the word?

The other body that Mr Miliband cited, the 'commission of bishops', was a little harder to identify, but patient research revealed that its full name was the 'Commission of Bishops' Conferences of the European Community' (COMECE). Far from being an episcopal body that just happened to back closer union, it was a Brussels-based outfit whose purpose was 'to promote reflection, based on the [Catholic] Church's social teaching, on the challenges facing a united Europe'.

In other words, while seeking to give the impression of broad support for a new transfer of powers to Brussels, the British foreign secretary was reduced to citing a body whose sole purpose is to interact with EU institutions, and which would be out of business if the EU disappeared. The French call the phenomenon *déformation professionelle*: the tendency, perhaps subliminally, to form opinions on the basis of what your job is.

These various front organizations can even be dragged into arguments between different EU institutions. When, for example, the European Commission sought new Continent-wide rules on pesticides in 2007, it set up an umbrella group called 'Pesticide Watch' – an amalgam of various EU-funded bodies – to push it in the direction it wanted. MEPs were then duly bombarded by emails from this campaign – presented, naturally, as missives from ordinary citizens.[6]

In much the same way, the Commission pays Friends of the Earth to urge it to take more powers in the field of climate change. It pays WWF to tell it to assume more control over environmental matters. It pays the European Trade Union Congress to demand more Brussels employment laws.

6 Speech to the European Parliament, Chris Heaton-Harris MEP, 27 October 2007

To summarize, the EU machine-guns cash at its client organizations, these organizations tell it what it wants to hear, and it then turns around and claims to have listened to The People. And here's the clever bit: millions are thereby drawn into the system, their livelihoods becoming dependent on the European project.

Back in 2003, when the European Constitution was first being drawn up, 200 organizations representing 'civil society' were invited to submit their suggestions on what it should contain. Interested in how these 200 bodies had been selected, I put down a written question asking which of them received grants from the EU. After some toing and froing, the answer eventually came back: all of them.

You see how the system works? The EU sets up and funds an interest group. That group duly demands that Eurocrats seize more powers. Eurocrats then announce that, in response to popular demand, they are extending their jurisdiction.

Virtually every field of activity has some approved, EU-sponsored pressure group to campaign for deeper integration: the European Union of Journalists, the European Women's Lobby, the European Cyclists' Federation. These are not independent associations which just happen to be in receipt of EU funds. They are, in most cases, creatures of the European Commission, wholly dependent on Brussels for their existence.

We can be pretty certain that the organizations in receipt of Brussels cash will be in the forefront of the UK's 'Remain' campaign. And by no means only the NGOs. The Confederation of British Industry (CBI), which has become essentially a pro-EU pressure group, has received 936,272 euros. UK Universities, which campaigns strenuously for the EU, frankly admits that 'EU funding is too important to be sacrificed'. And you can almost see its point: since 2008, British universities have had 889,889,754 euros from Brussels.

What UK Universities won't tell you is that all this money was, in effect, deducted from Britain's contribution to the EU. If Britain withdrew, it could make an equivalent or larger payment directly rather than routing it through Brussels. Alternatively, if there were advantages of scale in these international collaborations – as opposed to advantages to the officials who administer the grants – then the UK could remain involved with the EU funding programme in the way that non-EU Norway, Canada and Israel do. All three of these states participate in the EU's main international research programme, Horizon, on the same basis as the twenty-eight EU members. Indeed, one reason that Norway pays more than twice as much per head into the EU as Iceland does, despite the two states having near-identical deals with Brussels, is that it likes to opt in to common projects of this sort.

It was the Nobel Prize-winning economist Milton Friedman who coined the phrase 'the tyranny of the status quo'. What a brilliantly perceptive line. The tyranny of the status quo does not just refer to the fact that human beings are change-averse, though we are. It refers, also, to the way in which a corpus of vested interests grows up around whatever happens to be the established settlement.

Some of those fighting hardest to remain in the EU have strong personal reasons for doing so. A few of them are Eurocrats or former Eurocrats, but many more are benefiting from the system at second-hand. The local government Europe officers; the financial regulators whose bread-and-butter work is the enforcement of EU rules; the representatives of the professional associations and trade unions that maintain a presence in Brussels; the bureaucrats who flit between their national civil services and lucrative Brussels secondments; the Jean Monnet professors, whose chairs are endowed by the EU; the think-tanks that are contracted by the EU to carry out research projects on remarkably generous terms; the NGOs and charities in receipt of grants; the international aid consultants; the lobbyists, for whom the EU is a goldmine.

There are, of course, individuals in all these roles who put principle before *déformation professionelle* – class traitors, so to speak. But most people respond to incentives, and we can hardly blame them. It is usually a quite unconscious process. Even in their private moments, the recipients of EU largesse rarely verbalize the thought they mustn't vote against their benefactor; rather, they become subliminally receptive to arguments that Britain ought to have influence in Brussels, that the nation-state is passé and that the economy benefits from the EU.

I have seen it happen again and again in Brussels. Many MEPs are elected without strong views about European integration. A handful are even Eurosceptics. But, as their lips clamp around the teat of the expenses, their views shift. An MEP who, without doing anything improper, makes full use of his allowances will take home, net, considerably more than the British prime minister. A study in 2010 showed that more than a thousand Eurocrats, by no means all of them senior, also earn more than David Cameron.

An official working for an EU institution is exempt from national taxation, paying instead a token rate of EU tax equivalent to around 21 per cent, flat. Some member states recoup the difference from their MEPs, and some don't.

Ponder, for a moment, that extraordinary fact. The bureaucrats in the Commission and Parliament make decisions that have fiscal consequences for ordinary people, while themselves being exempt from those consequences. When we consider the oddities of the French *ancien régime*, one of the greatest iniquities, to modern eyes, is that the aristocracy was largely exempt from taxation. We wonder at a system based on the legal and systematic expropriation by the rich of the poor. Yet we have re-created such a system in Brussels.

The tax exemption is only the most visible and flagrant example; in truth, the entire EU system is based around transferring wealth from ordinary citizens to those lucky enough to be part of the machine.

This is perhaps less shocking than it sounds. Formalized confiscation is, historically, the usual form of human organization. The idea that a society should be run by and for the general population, rather than in the interests of its oligarchs, is a rare and recent one. In their great study, *Why Nations Fail*, James A. Robinson and Daron Acemoğlu showed that, in almost every age and nation, the people in power arrange things so that they and their heirs can systematically enjoy the fruits of everyone else's work. They call this model the 'extractive state'. The alternative – the rule of law, secure property rights and mechanisms to hold rulers to account – came about only in modern times and largely in English-speaking countries, though it later spread. This they call the 'inclusive state'.

As individual countries, the twenty-eight members of the EU qualify as inclusive states. They are parliamentary democracies with independent judiciaries; they do not systematically expropriate their citizens, intern without trial or forbid emigration; they recognize civil rights and equality before the law.

But what of the EU as such? It is hardly democratic; it rarely allows the dots and commas of the law to stand in the way of what it wants; and it certainly doesn't elevate individual freedom over collective interest. Sure, it's not a dictatorship, either: it doesn't take away our passports or throw us into gulags. But can it be called an inclusive state?

3

WHY THE EU CAN'T
BE DEMOCRATIC

O N 18 APRIL 1951, in the French foreign ministry's imposing Salon de l'Horloge, six men gathered to sign an accord unlike any other. The Treaty of Paris, which created the European Coal and Steel Community – the first direct ancestor of today's European Union – would not just bind its members as states. Rather, it would create a new legal order, superior to national jurisdictions.

The six men were the foreign ministers of the founding EEC members: Belgium, Luxembourg, the Netherlands, France, Italy and West Germany. This was the first treaty to which West Germany, recently under Allied occupation, had acceded in her own name, and her Chancellor, Konrad Adenauer, was there in person, acting as his own foreign minister.

When the time came for the formal signing, though, a problem arose. Last-minute negotiations and amendments meant that no official text had been prepared. The six ministers therefore signed an empty piece of paper, and left their officials to fill in the articles. As one historian of the EU puts it: 'The spirit of the accord stood surety for the letter.'[7]

To British eyes, it is an almost perfect symbol for what has been wrong with the European project from the beginning. The politicians have left the bureaucrats with, figuratively if not always literally, a series of blank sheets. The bureaucrats, unsurprisingly, have filled in the blanks to suit themselves. Again and again, the Brussels institutions have set aside both public opinion and the clear instructions of the member states in order to advance their agenda of 'more Europe'.

We tend to take the rule of law for granted. Those four words slide so easily from our tongues that we rarely stop to consider the vastness of what they represent. When the people in charge can no longer make up the rules as they go along, much follows: free contract, free conscience, free speech and, ultimately, prosperity,

7 *The Passage to Europe: How a Continent Became a Union* by Luuk van Middelaar, Yale (2013)

democracy and meritocracy. If one thing distinguishes, in Robinson and Acemoğlu's formulation, inclusive from extractive states, it is the elevation of the rules above the rulers.

So, does the EU qualify as an inclusive state? It certainly qualifies as, if not quite a state in the conventional sense, certainly a polity. Supporters of deeper integration have not yet fulfilled their ambition to create a country called Europe; but, over the past thirty years, they have bestowed on the EU many of the defining characteristics of nationhood: a currency, a criminal justice system, a president, a foreign minister, legal personality, treaty-making powers, common citizenship, a passport, a flag, an anthem. And they remain intent on completing the process. As Angela Merkel puts it: 'We need a political union, which means we must cede powers to Europe and give Europe control.'[8]

But, if the EU comes close to qualifying as a state, it falls well short of being law-based. Again and again, the treaties have been set aside for the sake of deeper union. The jurisdiction of the EU institutions is extended by judicial activism, without democratic consent. The rules are applied one-sidedly and arbitrarily to advance the goal of political amalgamation.

8 *Financial Times*, 7 June 2012

To cite only the most flagrant recent example, the eurozone bailouts were patently illegal. I don't just mean that they had no legal basis in the treaties; I mean that they were expressly prohibited. Article 125 of the EU Treaty is unequivocal: 'The Union shall not be liable for, or assume the commitments of, central governments, regional, local or other public authorities, other bodies governed by public law, or public undertakings of any Member State.'

This clause was no mere technicality. It was on the basis of its promise that the Germans agreed to join the euro in the first place. As Angela Merkel put it in 2010: 'We have a Treaty under which there is no possibility of paying to bail out states.'

Yet, as soon as it became clear that the euro wouldn't survive without cash transfusions, the treaties were set aside. Christine Lagarde, then the French finance minister, positively boasted about what had happened: 'We violated all the rules because we wanted to close ranks and really rescue the euro zone. The Treaty of Lisbon was very straightforward. No bailouts.'[9]

To British eyes, the whole process seemed bizarre. Rules had been drawn up in the clearest language that lawyers could devise. Yet, the moment they became inconvenient, they were ignored. When the London

9   Reuters, 18 December 2010

press said so, though, it was widely mocked for its insular, Anglo-Saxon literal-mindedness. Everyone else could see that, as a Portuguese MEP put it to me at the time, 'the facts matter more than the legislation'.

Without the rule of law, there is no representative government. There may be elections and referendums, but they will be swatted aside if they go the 'wrong' way.

Consider the way in which Brussels reacts when a national referendum goes against deeper integration. Figure Three records the various 'No' votes around the EU since Denmark rejected the Maastricht Treaty in 1992.

It's not just that Eurocrats are ready to swat aside democratic outcomes; it's that they openly admit to it – revel in it, we might almost say. In the run-up to Greece's 2015 referendum on whether to continue with the disastrous bailout-and-borrow racket that had prevented a recovery, the president of the European Commission, Jean-Claude Juncker, spelt out the official doctrine with brutal honesty: 'There can be no democratic choice against the European Treaties.'[10]

Mr Juncker was restating the long-standing Brussels doctrine that European integration matters more than how people vote. His predecessor, José Manuel Durão Barroso, used to contend that

10 *Le Figaro*, 28 January 2015

Fig. 3

DON'T TAKE NO
FOR AN ANSWER

Country	Date	Issue	'No' vote	Outcome
Denmark	1992	Maastricht Treaty	51.7%	Made to vote again
Denmark	2000	Joining the euro	53.2%	Accepted
Ireland	2001	Nice Treaty	53.9%	Made to vote again
Sweden	2003	Joining the euro	56.1%	Accepted
France	2005	EU Constitution	54.9%	Ignored
Netherlands	2005	EU Constitution	61.5%	Ignored
Ireland	2008	Lisbon Treaty	53.2%	Made to vote again
Greece	2015	Euro bailout	61.3%	Ignored

nation-states were dangerous precisely because they were democratic:

'Governments are not always right. If governments were always right we would not have the situation that we have today. Decisions taken by the most democratic institutions in the world are very often wrong.'[11]

There is an old joke in Brussels to the effect that, if the EU were a country applying to join itself, it would be rejected on grounds of being insufficiently democratic. The joke understates the magnitude of the problem. The Union is contemptuous of public opinion, not by some oversight but as an ineluctable consequence of its supranational nature.

The EU is run, extraordinarily, by a body that combines legislative and executive power. The European Commission is not only the EU's 'government'; it is also, in most fields of policy, the only body that can propose legislation. Such a concentration of power is itself objectionable enough; but what is truly extraordinary is that the twenty-eight commissioners are unelected.

Many supporters of the EU acknowledge this flaw. They call it the EU's 'democratic deficit', and vaguely admit that something ought to be done about it. But the democratic deficit isn't an accidental design-flaw; it is intrinsic to the whole project.

11 Speech in Berlin, 9 November 2011

The EU's founding fathers had had a mixed experience with democracy – especially the populist and plebiscitary strain that came into vogue between the wars. Too much democracy was associated, in their minds, with demagoguery and fascism. There were, of course, differences of emphasis among them. The scheming Jean Monnet, who was never elected to public office, was more suspicious of the ballot box than his ascetic countryman Robert Schuman, who was twice prime minister of France. Nonetheless, it is fair to say that the Euro-patriarchs prided themselves on creating a system where supreme power would be in the hands of 'experts': disinterested technocrats immune to the ballot box.

They understood very well that a scheme as audacious as theirs, the merging of ancient kingdoms and republics into a single state, would never succeed if each successive transfer of power from the national capitals to Brussels had to be approved by the voters. They were therefore quite unapologetic about designing a mechanism whereby public opinion would be tempered or moderated by a bureau of wise men.

Thus, from the beginning, the EU was built on undemocratic foundations. Public opinion was and is regarded as an obstacle to overcome, not a reason to change direction. Determined not to concede an inch

– or, rather, a centimetre – to voters who wanted less integration, Eurocrats were prepared, if necessary, simply to deny their existence. When France and the Netherlands voted against the European Constitution in 2005, Mr Juncker, then prime minister of Luxembourg, told MEPs: 'the French and Dutch did not really vote "No" to the European Constitution'.[12]

As in any abusive relationship, the contemptuous way in which Eurocrats treated voters became self-reinforcing. The more voters were ignored, the more cynical and fatalistic they became. They began to abstain in record numbers, complaining – quite under-standably – that it made no difference how they cast their ballots. Eurocrats, for their part, were obliged to construct a world-view that justified their readiness to defy the verdict of the urns. The imperatives of European integration required them to disregard popular majorities on the narrow issue of the EU; but this soon developed into a wider distrust of the masses.

Not all Eurocrats are cynics, of course. There are some idealists within the system: committed Euro-federalists who believe that it is possible to democratize the EU without destroying it. Their ideal is a pan-European democracy, based on a more powerful European Parliament. The model has been set out

12 *Daily Telegraph*, 17 July 2005

many times, most recently by Jean-Claude Juncker in his campaign to become president of the Commission in 2014. The European Commission would become the cabinet; the Council of Ministers would become the *Bundesrat* or upper house, representing the nation-states; and the European Parliament would become the main legislative body. It is hardly a new scheme. These were, indeed, the three specific proposals, put forward by Jacques Delors as long ago as 1990, that prompted Margaret Thatcher's famous response: 'No! No! No!'

Give MEPs more power, runs the theory, and people will take them more seriously. A higher calibre of candidate will stand, and turnout will rise. Pan-European political parties will contest the elections on common and binding manifestos. People will add a European dimension to their political identity. It will, at this stage, no longer be necessary for Eurocrats to swat aside referendum results or impose policies without popular consent because European democracy will have become a reality.

The problem with this idea is that it has already been tried. Its failure can be inferred empirically from the turnout rates.

Of those Europeans who had taken the trouble to register to vote before the 2014 elections to the European Parliament, no fewer than 57.5 per cent declined to cast their ballots on the day. The figure is all the more remarkable when we consider that voting is compulsory in some member states, that others sought to boost participation by holding municipal elections on the same day, and that Brussels spent hundreds of millions of euros on a campaign to encourage turnout.

Not that the abstention rate should have surprised anyone. As we can see in Figure Four, there has been an unbroken decline in turnout since the first elections to the European Parliament were held in 1979.

These statistics are a serious embarrassment for Euro-integrationists. In the early days, they used to argue that the high abstention rate was a consequence of unfamiliarity, a function of the relative powerlessness of the new institution.

That theory has now been comprehensively disproved. Over the past thirty-five years, the European Parliament – like the EU in general – has been steadily agglomerating powers. Yet people have responded by refusing to dignify it with their votes. The more familiar people have become with the EU, the further turnout has fallen.

MEPs, naturally enough, respond to each new low by, in effect, blaming the electorate. They demand better information campaigns, more extensive (and expensive) propaganda. Europe, they declare, matters

Fig. 4

MORE EUROPE,
LESS DEMOCRACY

European election year	Turnout
1979	62.0%
1984	59.0%
1989	58.4%
1994	56.7%
1999	49.5%
2004	45.6%
2009	43.1%
2014	42.5%

Source: European Parliament

more than ever and voters must be made to see it! It never occurs to them to infer any loss of legitimacy from the turnout figures, nor to devolve powers to a level of government that continues to enjoy democratic support. It is hard not to think of Bertolt Brecht's eerie lines: 'Wouldn't it therefore be easier to dissolve the people and elect another in their place?'

It won't do to claim that turnout is falling in every democracy. It isn't. In the US, for example, it rose from 49 per cent in 1996 to 55 per cent in 2012. Turnout at European elections is far lower than at national elections in the same countries, and is falling faster. Falling, we might add, for the most obvious of reasons: very few people think of themselves as Europeans in the same sense that they might think of themselves as Hungarian or Portuguese or Swedish. There is no pan-European public opinion, there are no pan-European media. You can't decree a successful democracy by bureaucratic fiat. You can't fabricate a sense of common nationality.

And yet, in a collective suspension of disbelief, the European elites are behaving as though a sense of European patriotism, or at least of unified identity, already existed. At the 2014 European election, the main political groups in the European Parliament agreed – and got those of their supporters who were also national leaders to agree too – that whichever group won the most MEPs would get to pick the next president of the European Commission.

Never mind that most voters are unaware of the existence of these transnational parties – the European People's Party, the Alliance of Liberals and Democrats for Europe, and so on. Never mind that a European election is, in reality, twenty-eight miniature referendums on twenty-eight national governments. Never mind that it is almost inconceivable that someone would say (for example) 'I voted for the Irish branch of the Party of the European Left' rather than 'I voted for Sinn Féin'.

The pan-European parties went along with the absurd pretence that people were voting for their Commission nominees. To see quite how unreal the whole process was, try to imagine any ordinary voter, in any EU state, saying: 'I was leaning towards Verhoftstadt but I think Juncker just edged the second TV debate.'

And yet no one stepped in to halt the charade. The European People's Party, which got the most seats, duly claimed victory on behalf of its candidate, Juncker. And, despite the furious opposition of David Cameron who pointed out (quite correctly) that the entire process was a power-grab by federalists that the nation-states had never consented to, Juncker was appointed.

His appointment was a huge advance for Euro-federalism. Although few of the heads of government liked or trusted Juncker, who had made many enemies while he was prime minister of Luxembourg, the member states went along with the ludicrous idea that he had somehow been elected by the people of Europe. Of the twenty-eight heads of government, only two – David Cameron and Hungary's Viktor Orbán – dissented. Euro-integrationists were ecstatic. Not only did Juncker share their view that the EU ought to be treated as a single country, but the manner of his appointment suggested that the national leaders, too, accepted at least part of that argument.

The trouble was that, outside Brussels, almost no one had heard of the languid Luxembourger. A survey of more than 12,000 people across the EU, carried out the week after the European election by Advanced Market Research, found that only 8.2 per cent of registered voters could identify Juncker.

A step forward for European democracy? Hardly. The same AMR poll showed that 91.2 per cent were unable to name any of the European political parties that claimed a mandate from the results – this despite the £52 million of European taxpayers' money allocated to those parties for the specific purpose of fighting the 2014 election, on top of their regular funds. In the United Kingdom, fewer than 1 per cent could name

Juncker, and the British party affiliated with his EPP secured just 0.18 per cent of the votes.

Elections alone do not make a democracy. There were regular elections in the Warsaw Pact states throughout the Cold War. There are elections in Iran today. For an election to matter, there has to be a meaningful engagement between voters and government. The EU, lacking a shared sense of common national identity, cannot fabricate such an engagement.

To put it another way, democracy requires a *demos*: a unit with which we identify when we use the word 'we'. Take away the *demos* and you are left only with the *kratos*: the power of a state that must compel by force of law what it cannot ask in the name of civic patriotism.

In the absence of a *demos*, governments are even likelier than usual to purchase votes through, for example, public works schemes and sinecures. Unable to draw upon any natural, patriotic loyalty, they have to buy the support of their electorates. One way to think of the EU is as a massive vehicle for the redistribution of wealth. Taxpayers in the states contribute (though their contributions are hidden among the national tax-takes) and the revenue is then used to purchase the allegiance of articulate and powerful groups: consultants, contractors, big landowners, NGOs, corporations, charities, municipalities.

So far, so familiar. The undemocratic nature of the Brussels institutions has been a Eurosceptic complaint from the beginning. What is much less widely appreciated is the extent to which, as well as being undemocratic within its own structures, the EU tends also to subvert the internal democracy of its member nations.

Consider a few examples. Ireland used to have exemplary laws on the conduct of referendums, providing for equal airtime for both sides and the distribution of a leaflet with the 'Yes' and 'No' arguments to every household. When these rules produced a 'No' to the Nice Treaty in 2001, they were revised so as to make it easier for the pro-EU forces to win a second referendum. That victory was duly secured, but a result was that all subsequent Irish referendums, not simply those to do with the EU, were fought on an unbalanced basis.

The same is true of Croatia, which dropped the minimum threshold provisions in its referendum rules in order to ensure entry into the EU in 2011.

When the president of the Czech Republic, Václav Klaus, declared that he was reluctant to sign the Lisbon Treaty into law, he was threatened with impeachment. He duly climbed down and, with poor grace, scrawled his name across the Bill; but, again, think of the precedent. From now on, any Czech president might face impeachment, not for impropriety, malfeasance or mental incapacity, but for sticking to the promises that he had very clearly made in the run-up to his election.

When Ireland's referendum on the Lisbon Treaty was announced, the European establishment required the taoiseach, Bertie Ahern, to stand aside lest the corruption allegations swirling around him destabilized the 'Yes' campaign. He was duly replaced with the most pro-EU member of his government, Brian Cowen. Cowen went on to lose anyway and then – in a move much applauded in Brussels – sided with the European Commission against his own electorate, demanding that people vote a second time. Once again, the EU got its way, in the sense that Ireland reversed its decision. But the price paid by Cowen's party was devastating.

Until the second Lisbon referendum, Fianna Fáil had been the fixed point in Ireland's party system, the star around which other parties orbited. It had won – in the sense of getting more votes than anyone else – every election since 1932, typically securing between 40 and 50 per cent of all ballots cast. In the 2011 general election, its share of the vote went from 41.6 per cent to 17.4 per cent, as voters turned against a government that had meekly agreed to the EU's loans-for-austerity deal, saddling them with the cost of propping up a chunk of the European banking system.

The distortion of Ireland's democracy was just the beginning. November 2011 witnessed Brussels-backed coups in two EU member states – bloodless and genteel coups, to be sure, but coups nonetheless. In Greece and in Italy, elected prime ministers were toppled and replaced with Eurocrats – respectively a former vice-president of the European Central Bank, Lucas Papademos, and a former European Commissioner, Mario Monti.

The two premiers, George Papandreou in Greece and Silvio Berlusconi in Italy, had inadvertently stumbled into the path of the EU's combine harvester. Papandreou's mistake was to call for a referendum on Greece's austerity deal – a move which prompted purple, choking fury in Brussels where, as we have seen, the first rule is 'no referendums'.

Papandreou was not a Eurosceptic. On the contrary, he fervently wanted Greece to stay in the euro and had planned to campaign for a 'Yes' vote. His sin, in the eyes of the Brussels establishment, was not to hold the wrong opinions, but to be too keen on democracy. Leninists had a term for party members who, though committed Bolsheviks, nonetheless behaved in a way that jeopardized the movement. They were called 'objectively counter-revolutionary'. Papandreou's reckless desire to consult the voters put him in this category; four days later, he was out.

Berlusconi, too, got on the wrong side of the EU. His pronouncement that 'since the introduction of the euro, most Italians have become poorer' was factually true, but sealed his fate. At a meeting in Frankfurt's opera house, Nicolas Sarkozy, Angela Merkel, Jean-Claude Juncker and the leaders of the IMF and ECB decided that the Italian premier was an obstacle to their plan to keep the euro together. We can hardly call it a secret plot: at the Cannes summit a few days later, officials were proudly wearing badges proclaiming their membership of the 'Frankfurt Group'. One such official happily declared: 'We're on our way to moving out Berlusconi'.[13] If this was a conspiracy, it was what H. G. Wells called 'an open conspiracy'. Sure enough, a few days later, Berlusconi was gone, his exit triggered by a combination of a sudden withdrawal of ECB support for Italian bonds, verbal attacks from other EU leaders and a rebellion from Europhile Italian MPs.

It is true, of course, that both Papandreou and Berlusconi were already unpopular for domestic reasons – just as Margaret Thatcher had been when EU leaders and Conservative Euro-enthusiasts joined forces

13 *The Spectator*, 12 November 2011

to bring her down in November 1990. Had they been at the height of their powers, they would not have been vulnerable. Nonetheless, to depose an incumbent head of government, even a wounded one, is no small thing.

Silvio Berlusconi, in particular, had survived a series of blows that would have felled anyone else. He had weathered accusations of bribery, soliciting underage sex, tax fraud and mafia links. He had shrugged off the attentions of – by his own count – 789 prosecutors and magistrates. He had laughed off gaffes on electric-rail topics from Muslims to Nazis. But he could not withstand the EU.

With Papandreou and Berlusconi out of the way, Brussels was able to install technocratic juntas in their place. Neither Lucas Papademos nor Mario Monti had ever stood for public office in his life. Mr Monti, indeed, managed to fill his entire cabinet without appointing a single elected politician. Both men headed what were called 'national governments' but these administrations had been called into being solely to enforce programmes that their nations had rejected. Both men derived their real mandates from their support in Brussels, and everyone knew it.

The most shocking aspect of the whole affair was that so few people were shocked. Two countries which, in living memory, had emerged from dictatorship were now suspending multi-party democracy. True, the outward forms of constitutionalism were observed: both new regimes were formally endorsed by parliamentary votes. Similar things could be said, though, of almost every tyrant in history, from Bonaparte onwards. The fact remained that these regimes existed for the narrow and explicit purpose of implementing policies that their peoples would throw out at a general election.

The Brussels system had been undemocratic from the start but its hostility to the ballot box had always been disguised by the outward trappings of constitutional rule in its member nations. In 2011, that ceased to be true. *Apparatchiks* in Brussels now ruled directly through apparatchiks in Athens and Rome. The voters and their tribunes were cut out altogether. There was no longer any pretence.

One of the ousted leaders was from the Centre-Left, the other from the Centre-Right. As you might expect, in each case, supporters of the deposed premier complained while his opponents cheered. But very few people made the case in principle that it was wrong for Brussels to connive at the overthrow of an elected national leader.

The silence on the democratic Left was especially puzzling. Perhaps the Left's proudest boast and finest achievement is that it has spread power from oligarchs to ordinary people. Yet although plenty of individual Leftists decried what was happening, the main social-democratic parties around Europe fell in behind an essentially elitist and anti-democratic manoeuvre.

For Britain's Labour Party, it represented the culmination of a shift that had been taking place since the 1960s. The reason that the United Kingdom had not been present at that meeting in the Salon de l'Horloge in 1951 was that the post-war Labour government saw itself as being engaged in a long-overdue dispersal of power away from élites, and had no intention of doing the opposite at European level. Clement Attlee, then prime minister, declared that he would never accept that 'the most vital economic forces of this country should be handed over to an authority that is utterly undemocratic and accountable to nobody'.

Democratic accountability was at the heart of Labour Euroscepticism throughout the 1960s and 1970s. The far-Left firebrand Tony Benn explained why in his diary following a visit to Brussels as a minister in 1974:

> This huge Commission building in Brussels, in the shape of a cross, is absolutely un-British. I felt as if I were going as a slave to Rome; the whole relationship was wrong. Here was I, an elected man who could be removed, doing a job, and here were these people with

more power than I had and no accountability to any-
body. My visit confirmed in a practical way all my
suspicions that this would be the decapitation of British democracy without any countervailing advantage,
and the British people, quite rightly, wouldn't accept
it. There is no real benefit for Britain.

Euroscepticism remained the mainstream Labour position until 1988, when Jacques Delors, then president
of the European Commission, won over the Trades
Union Congress by promising that the EU would
guarantee the social and employment rights that the
Thatcher administration saw as burdensome.

Oddly, very few trade unionists made the democratic
objection to that argument, namely that, while the
EU might mean more employment regulations today,
it might equally mean fewer regulations tomorrow,
and voters would have lost their ability to do anything
about it. As Tony Benn used to put it: 'I'd rather have
a bad parliament than a good king.'

Even more oddly, the Euroscepticism of the
democratic Left evaporated just as its prescience was
being demonstrated. The year 2015 saw precisely
what Tony Benn had warned against: the overruling
of an elected Leftist government, which had clear
public support, by the Brussels bureaucracy. The EU

prevented Alexis Tsipras, Greece's radical new prime minister, from implementing the manifesto on which he had been elected.

As a Conservative, I had little sympathy for Mr Tsipras's agenda – although he was right to point to the insanity of requiring a country in Greece's situation to raise taxes while cutting spending. My sympathy, though, was hardly the point. Tsipras's party, Syriza, commanded a parliamentary majority, and the electorate explicitly re-endorsed its opposition to the bailout-and-borrow plan in a referendum. The EU responded by forcing Greece to accept worse terms than had been offered before the referendum. As Germany's finance minister, Wolfgang Schäuble, put it in December 2014: 'Elections change nothing.'

It was a vivid realization of Tony Benn's warnings from forty years earlier – though the old-fashioned English radical had sadly died a few months too soon to see his prophecies vindicated. His death also meant that he missed seeing another of his fears confirmed, namely the extent to which the EU's lack of democracy would open the door to corporate control.

4

EURO-CORPORATISM

IN SEPTEMBER 2015, the automobile industry was hit by the worst scandal in its history. It emerged that the German car-maker Volkswagen had been programming its vehicles to cheat emissions tests. Some of Volkswagen's diesel engines were fitted with a software-controlled device that detected the conditions of a laboratory test, and caused the emissions of nitrogen oxide (NO_2) to drop to as little as one-fortieth of what would be emitted on the open road.

The discovery was, of course, a terrible blow to the company. But it raised another question. Why had the EU, almost uniquely in the world, adopted standards that promoted diesel engines? While the American and

Japanese governments were encouraging hybrid and electric cars, the EU struck out in a very different direction, enforcing emissions standards that focused on carbon dioxide (CO_2) instead of nitrogen oxide.

The automotive diesel market was almost dead in the late 1980s, when Volkswagen revived the technology with its turbocharged direct injection (TDI) engines. European car manufacturers saw a market opportunity and set about lobbying for Brussels rules that would give them an advantage over their rivals. It wasn't an easy case to make. Diesel emits four times more NO_2 than petrol, and twenty-two times more particulates – the tiny pollutants that penetrate our lungs, brains and hearts. Most consumers still thought of diesel, with reason, as the dirtier alternative. How were car producers like BMW, Volkswagen and Daimler to ask for a protected market share?

Well, they were savvy enough not to put the argument in terms of their commercial self-interest. Instead, they focused on the need to reduce CO_2 emissions, and so slow climate change. Although diesel is the filthier fuel in most other respects, it does produce 15 per cent less CO_2 than petrol. And so a massive operation was begun to sell the new standard as part of the Kyoto process. Health risks were overlooked and the conversation was skilfully turned to global warming.

It worked. During the mid-1990s, the car companies negotiated a deal with the European Commission which prioritized a cut in CO_2 emissions over the more immediate health problems caused by exhaust fumes – an arrangement announced in 1998 by Neil Kinnock, then the transport commissioner. According to Simon Birkett of Clean Air London: 'It was practically an order to switch to diesel. The European car fleet was transformed from being almost entirely petrol to predominantly diesel. Britain, along with Germany, France and Italy, offered subsidies and sweeteners to persuade car makers and the public to buy diesel.'[14]

Although few remarked on it, that deal heralded a massive divergence between the EU's car market and the rest of the world's. 'It's fascinating that this essentially transformed the market in Europe and nobody paid attention to it,' says Eugenio J. Miravete, a professor of political economy at the University of Texas and co-author, with Maria J. Moral of UNED in Madrid and Jeff Thurk of the University of Notre Dame, of a study on the rise of the diesel car in Europe.[15]

The car companies' strategy was successful. Diesel went from less than 10 per cent of the UK market in

14 *Guardian*, 22 September 2015
15 'Innovation, emissions policy, and competitive advantage in the diffusion of European diesel automobiles', 30 September 2015

1995 to more than half in 2012, with equivalent rises in other EU states. Because the industry had been savvy enough to make its case in terms of climate change rather than commercial advantage, the ministers and pressure groups who might have been expected to scrutinize what was happening tended to give car-makers the benefit of the doubt – right up until the shock of the 2015 Volkswagen revelations.

Let's summarize what happened. The EU, lobbied by a vested interest, adopted rules that killed large numbers of European citizens. Yes, killed. We can't quantify the fatalities precisely because the cause of death in each case was recorded as cancer or heart failure rather than NO_2 inhalation or particulates emissions. But we are talking about thousands of need-less deaths: air pollution kills more people globally than malaria and HIV combined.

No one willed these deaths, of course. The ministers and policy-makers believed they were saving lives by tackling carbon emissions. At worst, they made a utilitarian trade-off. As a senior department of trans-port official later put it: 'To be totally reductionist, you are talking about killing people today rather than saving lives tomorrow.'[16] You could argue that politics is all about making unpleasant decisions, and neither

16 *Guardian*, 22 September 2015

that official nor anyone else knew that Volkswagen had found a way to get around the tests for which it had lobbied.

Nor, of course, were the car companies deliberately setting out to murder people. Their employees are no less subject to *déformation professionelle* than Eurocrats or, indeed, anyone else. It is only human to convince yourself of the morality of something that you happen to find convenient. Behavioural psychologists call it 'self-serving bias'. No doubt the Brussels-based lobbyists acting for the car giants genuinely convinced themselves that they were saving the planet.

Still, facts are facts. EU policy ended up killing many innocent people in the commercial interest of one industrial sector. That, surely, is as big a scandal as the test cheating itself.

Why do such things happen? To understand the answer, you need only spend a couple of weeks in the EU quarter in Brussels. Those grey, rainy streets are, to lobbying, what Silicon Valley is to hi-tech.

Lobbyists love the EU, intuiting from the moment they arrive that it was designed by and for people like them. There are some 25,000 lobbyists in Brussels, some in-house, some working for several clients, some representing pressure groups or regions, most representing big business. Figure Five shows the industries that have invested most heavily in purchasing face-time, but it is only fair to record that Big Oil and Big Pharma have their equivalents on the other side: Greenpeace and the WWF spent a million euros each during the same six-month period, and Oxfam managed 300,000 euros (a pretty good investment when we consider the vast millions it gets from Brussels in grants).

What all these lobbies have in common, whether industrial or environmental, is a preference for corporatism and back-room deals. The EU has a special name for the procedure by which it makes law: 'comitology'. Committees and technical experts meet and make trade-offs out of the public eye. Such a system is an invitation to lobbyists and pressure groups to reach arrangements behind closed doors that might not look very pretty if the details were known.

One example will serve as an illustration of what I'm talking about. Starting in 2005, the EU began to regulate, and in some cases ban outright, a number of higher-dose vitamin and mineral supplements, herbal remedies and other alternative medicines.

Its motive was far from obvious to the casual observer. Twenty million citizens around the EU were making either frequent or occasional use of the targeted products, and there was no evidence that they were deleterious to health.

Fig. 5

BIG
SPENDERS

Name of company	Lobbying budget, first half of 2015 (euros)
Microsoft Corporation	4,500,000
Shell Companies	4,500,000
ExxonMobil Petroleum & Chemical	4,500,000
Deutsche Bank AG	3,962,000
Dow Europe GmbH	3,750,000
Google	3,500,000
General Electric Company (GE)	3,250,000
Siemens AG	3,230,169
Huawei Technologies	3,000,000
BP	2,500,000

Source: Transparency International

Opinion was and is divided about the efficacy of complementary medicine – in my family as elsewhere. I take the view that most of these products are harmless placebos, while my wife sees them as an important part of a holistic approach to health.

It's generally a good strategy to listen to your wife. 'Better is a dinner of herbs where love is, than a stalled ox and hatred therewith,' says the Book of Proverbs – and rarely could the bit about the herbs have applied so literally as in this instance. In any case, Mrs Hannan is far from unusual in her views. In sixteen years as an MEP, I have never had so many letters and emails from worried constituents. It struck me that, whatever the scientific arguments, this was a straightforward case of defending freedom.

But I was puzzled. Why did the EU want to ban or restrict substances that were at best health-giving and at worst harmless? Why was it alienating health shop owners and their customers all over Europe? Supporters of the regulation liked to cite 'the precautionary principle' but, deep down, they knew that they were putting herbalists in the impossible position of having to prove a negative. There ought to be such a thing as the presumption of innocence, in commerce as in criminal justice. No herbalist sets out to poison her clients: it's a poor business model. Regulation should be brought in only proportionately and where there is an identified need.

In this case, no such need could be established. Of course, Eurocrats are rarely bothered by proportionality. In their view, 'unregulated' is synonymous with 'illegal'. The idea that an absence of regulation might be the natural state of affairs finds little sympathy in the EU. British herbalists had been essentially self-regulating since a dispensation dating from the reign of Henry VIII, which gave them the freedom to trade without being prosecuted for witchcraft. In Brussels, this was regarded, not as an ancient liberty, but as a loophole that needed closing.

Some of the large pharmaceutical companies, well understanding the Eurocrat mind-set, saw an opportunity to put their smaller rivals out of business. The new legislation required expensive tests that were beyond the means of small producers. The big companies, which had entire compliance departments, were able to meet the new costs without difficulty. As independent herbalists reduced the range of what they could sell, and in some cases went out of business altogether, the giants assumed a larger market share.

Now who gained from that procedure and who lost? The multi-nationals did very well out of it, obviously, and consumers did badly. But the European economy as a whole suffered, too. Whenever a cartel of large companies succeeds in raising barriers to entry, the climate becomes less congenial to start-ups, and some entrepreneurs take their energy elsewhere.

Lobbying is not unique to Brussels but it is worth asking whether legislation of this kind would have passed through the (then) twenty-five national legislatures. I doubt it. Across Europe, MPs were deluged, just as I was, with letters from the users of alternative medicines who feared that the new restrictions would harm their health. But the decision was not in the hands of those national legislators. It was made by the unelected Commission and approved by the European Parliament – whose members, as we have seen, are remote to the point of near-invisibility.

One of the reasons that the EU is stagnating while other advanced economies grow is because cronyism and protectionism flourish in the necessarily undemocratic Brussels institutions.

To return one last time to the Robinson/Acemoğlu definition, a distinctive feature of an extractive state is hostility to new technology. Existing elites fear, with reason, that the creative destruction of new inventions might jeopardize their position. They therefore lobby to keep things more or less as they are.

In the twenty-eight member states, this isn't always

easy. The individual nations are democracies with independent judiciaries: inclusive states. But in the EU, whose institutions were designed by men who distrusted democracy, it is far easier to reach cosy accommodations with decision-makers. The system is a paradise for vested interests, and vested interests rarely like innovation.

Philippe Legrain, a Europhile who used to advise José Manuel Barroso at the Commission, has honestly diagnosed the problem:

> Traditional media companies, such as the Axel Springer group, resent their reliance on Google to drive traffic to their sites and its ability to sell advertising based on snippets of their content. Part-state-owned Deutsche Telekom hates that its customers use its network to make calls on Skype, send messages on WhatsApp and watch videos on Netflix and YouTube, without it earning additional revenues from those services. TUI, the world's largest travel agency and tour operator, feels threatened by TripAdvisor. Retailers fear Amazon's ever-expanding empire. Germany's mighty industrial lobby frets that American tech companies could eat their manufacturing lunch.

In fairness, European businesses are not alone in disliking competition. All big companies fear rivals and crave monopolies. Few if any mega-corporations are run by doctrinaire free-marketeers. Multi-national giants will naturally attempt, to the extent that they can get away with it, to rig the rules in their own favour.

What is unique about the EU is not that it has some peculiar predisposition to corporatism. The corporatist – the networking, name-dropping Davos Man – can be found in every company and on every continent. No, the peculiar characteristic of the EU is that its institutions are removed from the public. Legrain again:

> The Commission is launching a 'comprehensive investigation' into the role of internet platforms, such as search engines, online marketplaces, social networks, app stores and services in the sharing economy. Almost all of these happen to be American: think Google, Amazon, Facebook, Apple and Uber. As the EU's digital commissioner, Günther Oettinger, put it at the launch of the DSM strategy, the EU needs to regain its 'digital independence'.

If you want an explanation for the EU's sluggish growth, look no further. As Berin Szoka of the think-tank TechFreedom puts it: 'Europe has a collective insecurity complex about the Internet.'[17]

17 TechFreedom post, 15 December 2015

Brussels is by no means the only place where a mild suspicion of democracy goes hand-in-hand with a dislike of an essentially bottom-up, unguided mechanism like the Web. The trouble is that every new directive, from the attempt to regulate bloggers as if they were newspapers to the ham-fisted data protection rules, tends to hurt start-ups. As Szoka says: 'Regulatory discretion is used as a rule of digital protectionism, and Europe falls further and further behind Silicon Valley.'

To repeat, national regulators can also be change-averse, heavy-handed and prone to lobbying from vested interests. But the problem is proportionate to the distance between government and governed. The more remote the institutions, the more prone they become to producer-capture.

At the same time, the sheer diversity of conditions and needs across the EU guarantees that regulations have unintended consequences. The economy always suffers when an industrial cartel reaches a deal with government officials; but those who suffer most are those whose standards or products diverge most from the cartel's. The more pluralist an economy is, the more losers there will necessarily be when regulations are passed.

Again, one example will serve to demonstrate the phenomenon. At the time of writing, the EU is drawing up a directive that directly threatens the viability of Britain's commercial ports. Not from malice but simply because it is impossible to apply a one-size-fits-all policy to such a heterodox continent.

British ports are private, profitable and plentiful. They tend to be smaller than their Continental equivalents and are dotted more thickly along our coasts. British ports, unusually, don't rely on state aid, instead generating a healthy surplus for the Treasury and sustaining some 100,000 jobs.

The Continental model is very different. Ports on the other side of the Channel tend to be sparser and larger, and are generally either state-owned or dependent on grants. They are less likely than British ports, for reasons of geography, to compete with one another. The European Commission has therefore moved a regulation that would require them to introduce a measure of internal competition – in other words, to contract out their mooring, dredging, unloading, bunkering and so on to rival providers. The regulation also provides for the formal establishment of regulatory bodies: this is the EU, after all.

Now, there may be a case for more competition within such gigantic ports as Rotterdam and Antwerp. Even if there is, I'm not sure that it needs to come from Brussels, but let's leave that to one side; there is at least an argument to the effect that more diversity might lead to more efficiency and lower costs.

No such argument applies in the United Kingdom, where there is a thriving market, within which ports already compete against each other. Because our ports are relatively small, obligatory internal competition would wreck their economies of scale and deter investment. The companies that win the contracts for port services generally commit to major infrastructure costs: cranes, terminal facilities and the like. There is a widespread concern that the new rule – the Port Services Regulation – will kill such investment.

And here's the thing: no one really denies it. It's not just that all the British port operators and trade unions oppose the idea. You also won't find a single Commission official who thinks that the regulation will benefit Britain. Indeed, one senior Eurocrat privately told me that the measure was never intended to apply to small ports outside the state sector.

So why not simply amend the legislation so as to exempt privately-funded ports? An easy solution all round, you'd think. Except that the regulation has now become a battleground between those MEPs who want to retain generous state aid to their local ports (the MEP in charge of the bill, for example, represents Hamburg, which has had around a billion euros in subsidy since 2009) and those officials who want to reduce such grants. As long as that deadlock continues, no one wants to accept amendments about other things. Britain, in other words, is being held hostage in a wholly unrelated dispute.

It is just one episode, but it neatly illustrates the problem. Britain is adversely affected by Brussels rules that are not designed with her needs in mind, and can be outvoted even on matters where she has a vital national interest.

I chose the example of ports only because it is current. Art dealers, cheesemakers, temping agencies, slaughtermen, fund managers, trawlermen, steel workers, cider producers: all have suffered from EU rules designed to suit someone else. Of course, plenty of sectors in other EU states have suffered similarly from regulations that took no account of their conditions. Yet, oddly, it seems to happen rather more often to British firms. It's worth exploring why this should be.

5

BRITAIN'S LACK OF INFLUENCE

THE FALL-BACK POSITION of EU supporters, confronted with some indefensible Brussels policy, is to say: 'Well, that's something we ought to reform rather than just walking away.'

Brilliant! Reform! Why has no one thought of it before?

In fact, the story of the United Kingdom's involvement, first with the EEC, then the EC, now the EU, is a story of constant attempts at reform. You won't find many British politicians over the past fifty years, from any party, who openly favoured a United States of Europe. Almost all said that they wanted a Europe of nations – a flexible alliance of states, co-operating to achieve what they can't achieve singly, but ultimately responsible to their own democratic institutions.

If that model had ever been on offer, there would have been no argument and we wouldn't now be holding a referendum. You would have to be rather eccentric to object, in principle, to participating in a regional club committed to the promotion of trade and intergovernmental collaboration. The problem is that, while British politicians and writers have fantasized about a Europe of nations, the EU has steadily been moving in a different direction.

The referendum before us now – it seems odd that this needs stating but it evidently does – is about the EU that has in fact taken shape, not about some idealized version that we might have preferred.

The pattern has been the same from the beginning. Every British leader, at least since the 1960s, has come to office promising a fresh start in Europe. Every one has tried to win friends and gain influence by making some initial concessions. Each has found that the concessions are pocketed while the EU continues its stately march towards federal union.

The EEC that Britain joined in 1973 has since extended its jurisdiction, progressively, to foreign policy, environmental regulation, immigration, criminal justice and social policy. It has acquired, one by one, the accoutrements of statehood, from uniformed armed forces to a standardized driving licence. Now it aspires to a common tax and social security system, a federal police force and an army. And yet, all the while, successive British leaders have been singing the same song about a Europe of nations.

It started even before we joined. When Harold Macmillan launched our first application in 1961, he was already arguing that, by getting stuck in, he could turn the EEC away from political integration. A paper presented to the cabinet admitted that most Continental leaders wanted a political union but argued that 'the effects of any eventual loss of sovereignty would be mitigated if resistance to Federalism on the part of some of the governments continues, which our membership might be expected to encourage'.

Even in Macmillan's day, this was wishful thinking – although, with the EEC not yet five years old, it was perhaps excusable. It is less excusable today, after half a century during which the EEC, a common market, has been turned into the EU, a quasi-state. Yet still we delude ourselves, imagining that the other members are on the verge of coming round to our point of view.

The funny thing is that there is always some apparently plausible reason for thinking so. Every enlargement round, for example, was hailed as likely to lead to a looser Europe. Instead, the EU deepened each time it widened: the accession of Spain and Portugal in 1986 led directly to the Single European Act, that of the Nordic countries in 1994 to the Amsterdam Treaty, and that of the ex-Comecon states in 2004 to the Lisbon Treaty.

Alternatively, we are asked to believe that some change of government brings us an 'important ally'. Ludicrous as it now seems, Jacques Chirac, José María Aznar, Nicolas Sarkozy, Silvio Berlusconi, Donald Tusk and even Gerhard Schröder were all hailed in their time as leaders who would side with Britain against federalism.

Today we're told that the euro crisis has revealed the limits of integration, or that the collapse of Schengen heralds a return to the pre-eminence of national authorities. Some EU supporters have even taken to arguing that, since the whole structure is going to come tumbling down anyway, there is no need for Britain to make itself unpopular by walking out first.

It's a curious line to take: surely if you're in a structure that is about to come tumbling down, walking out is the prudent course. Be that as it may, though, there is no evidence that the EU's rush to closer union is slowing.

You might think that a logical response to the euro crisis would be to consider whether having a single currency was a mistake. Perhaps, if differing economies could not be jammed together without disproportionate cost, it might make sense to have a looser arrangement.

That, though, is not how the EU works. In Brussels, the euro crisis was seen, not as evidence that monetary union didn't work, but as evidence that it hadn't gone far enough. If monetary union was a failure, the EU must double down, adopting economic and fiscal union as well. A bailout fund was created, contrary to the letter and spirit of the treaties, but this wasn't enough. Eurocrats and MEPs began to demand debt-pooling, fiscal transfers, a shared finance ministry and, ultimately, EU taxes.

These are not the loopy ideas of a few fringe federalists. They are the road that the EU plainly intends to follow. As usual, it is advertising its intentions with admirable frankness; and, as usual, most British commentators are looking the other way.

On 22 June 2015, with much fanfare, the European Commission set out its scheme to acquire massive new powers in the wake of the euro crisis. 'Completing Europe's Economic and Monetary Union' was a comprehensive blueprint for what will happen next. The document is more commonly referred to as the

Five Presidents' Report, because all five of its nominal co-authors were presidents or ex-presidents of EU institutions.

The Five Presidents' Report makes abundantly clear that the travails of the euro are the business of all twenty-eight members, not just those that chose to abandon their national currencies. The plan for fiscal union will, it says, 'be developed within the framework of the European Union'.

And what form will this integration take? It won't just be about tax harmonization, though that is a large part of it. The Five Presidents make clear that they also intend to have 'deeper integration of national labour markets', greater 'co-ordination of social security systems', and to harmonize 'insolvency law', 'company law' and 'property rights'.

The United Kingdom will, of course, stand against all these things for a while, then be outvoted, and then sulkily go along with them. Such has been her story ever since she joined. Sometimes, she has slowed things up for a while. Sometimes, as on the Charter of Fundamental Rights, the Social Chapter or the 48-hour week, she has secured an opt-out, only for it to be struck down by the EU's authorities.

It seems clear that something similar will happen over the euro and Schengen. Although Britain will keep the pound, she is already being dragged into the bailouts, and will over time be part of a fiscal union. And although she will keep the physical right to police her frontiers, she has already lost the right to determine who can cross them.

The idea that 'Europe is coming round to the British point of view' is as wrong now as under any previous government. Since majority voting was introduced in the late 1980s, the UK has voted against an EU legislative proposal seventy times. She has lost the vote seventy times.

No other country is so regularly isolated and outvoted. Figure Six shows how many times each member state has been in the losing minority in formal votes in Council. These figures understate the problem since, by long-standing tradition, member states rarely force matters to a vote when they know they will lose. Even so, the raw numbers give a pretty good indication of the problem in proportionate terms.

These statistics comprehensively destroy the chief 'Remain' argument, namely that being in the EU gives Britain influence. In fact, despite being the second-largest financial contributor, she has very little influence when push comes to shove.

They also destroy the idea that qualified majority voting is a way to prise open markets, forcing

Fig. 6

INFLUENCE?
WHAT INFLUENCE?

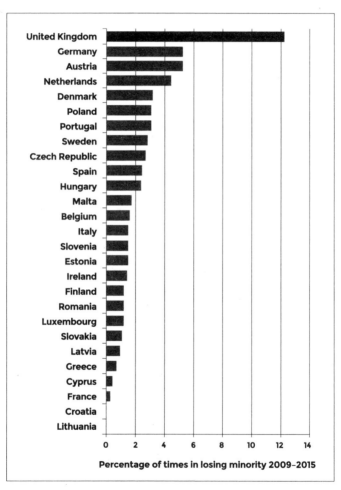

Percentage of times in losing minority 2009–2015

Source: European Council

competition on vested interests – the basis on which Margaret Thatcher accepted the idea. In fact, the abolition of the national veto has at least as often been used to impose a more dirigiste policy on Britain as a more open one on France.

Why, though, is Britain so often in a category of her own? Why does she have such little sway with the other states? Is it because Britons are naturally unpopular? Is there some Eurovision Song Contest-style prejudice against us? Are we resented, on some deep psychological level, for having won the Second World War?

It seems unlikely. Diplomatic trade-offs are made on the basis of present advantage, not past grudges or gratitude. No, there is a far simpler explanation. Britain is in a permanent minority because her interests and outlook diverge from the European mean more than those of any other state.

This is partly a question of economics. Britain differs cyclically and structurally from other EU economies. Her massive investments in and from the United States make her economy Atlantic rather than European, and her services sector has no equal on the Continent. In addition, as we have seen, she is one of only two member states that trade more outside the EU than inside it, and that disparity is growing.

The real difference, though, is one of what the Germans call *Weltanschauung* – a way of looking at the world. The United Kingdom did indeed stand slightly apart from Europe in 1945, in a way that was to define her relations with Brussels. She, alone, had come through the Second World War without, at any time, losing. In consequence, her political institutions – uniquely – were neither restored nor reinvented.

Across post-war Europe, there was a widespread sense that the nation-state had failed. Nationalism, in many Continental countries, had been tainted by fascism or collaboration or both. In Britain, unusually, patriotism had been a focus of resistance against the Nazi menace.

And, of course, Britain felt especially close, after 1945, to her Commonwealth allies who, rushing to the defence of the mother country, had left their dead all over Europe.

It was hardly surprising that such a Britain should have had little interest in the creation of a European federation. Or perhaps it would be more correct to say that Britain had little interest in joining such a federation. The general attitude at the time was that some sort of European political union might help the belligerents in the recent war to get over their differences. If the French, Germans and others decided to build common political structures, the thinking went, then Britain should support them from the outside, like a flying buttress on a mediaeval cathedral.

Euro-integrationists never tire of quoting Winston Churchill's call, at a speech in Zurich on 19 September 1946, for a 'United States of Europe'. But they rarely quote the next passage, in which he made clear that the United Kingdom would not be part of it:

> There is already a natural grouping in the Western Hemisphere. We British have our own Commonwealth of Nations. Why should there not be a European group which could give a sense of enlarged patriotism and common citizenship to the distracted peoples of this turbulent and mighty continent, and why should it not take its rightful place with other great groupings in shaping the destinies of men?

In case anyone had missed the point, Churchill ended with a call for Britain and the Commonwealth, along with the United States and perhaps even Russia, to 'be the friends and sponsors of the new Europe, and champion its right to live and shine'.

Britain's coolness toward Euro-federalism under Churchill, Attlee and Eden should not be taken for arrogance or stand-offishness. The United Kingdom was actively involved in the reconstruction of the war-ravaged continent. She took the lead in establishing the North Atlantic Treaty Organization (NATO), the Western European Union and the Council of Europe. She made a massive commitment to the defence of European democracy by stationing troops across West Germany and other frontline states. She voluntarily gave a portion of her Marshall Aid money and, indeed, of her rations, to help the people of Germany, who had come close to starvation.

British policy-makers hoped that the organization responsible for the distribution of America's Marshall Aid – then called the Organisation for European Economic Co-operation (OEEC), now the Organisation for Economic Co-operation and Development (OECD) – would form a broad, pan-European free trade area, linked to the United States: an economic branch of NATO, so to speak.

That view was not shared, however, by the leaders of other Western European countries. As far as they were concerned, the key aim was political unification, which they believed, sincerely if wrongly, to be the only correct response to the two dreadful wars through which they had lived. Hence their determination to begin with coal and steel – without which war was thought to be impossible.

Economics was subordinated to politics. To put it more plainly, economic integration was seen as a way to build a United States of Europe rather than as a way to make people better off. Right from the start, it was decided that a high tariff wall, along with a common industrial policy and a common agricultural policy, would mesh the participating states more closely together.

For free-trading Britain, with her global supply lines and her habit of importing food and commodities from the Commonwealth, such policies were unthinkable. She sought to separate the issue of commerce from that of political federation – that is, to encourage the countries that wanted to merge their institutions to do so within a broader pan-European free trade area. But her arguments served only to spur the federalists to greater haste.

There is a persistent myth that the EU developed in ways that were uncongenial to Britain because she made the mistake of standing aside at the beginning. Had Britain joined when the original Six came together, the argument goes, the entire EU might have developed in a less dirigiste, less protectionist and less integrationist manner. This argument was turned into a full-length book called *Missed Chances* by Sir Roy Denman, the official who eventually negotiated

Britain's accession in 1973 and went on to serve as the EU's representative in Washington. According to his thesis, now a mainstay of the pro-EU argument, Britain's 'delusions of grandeur' prevented her from getting involved politically in the nascent EEC and she has paid the price ever since.

The easiest way to refute this notion is to contrast Britain's continued isolation within the EU with that of the nineteen states that joined after she did. Plainly, if early membership were the key to influence, Britain would be far more influential, relative to her size and population, than Slovenia or Sweden or Spain. In fact, as the renegotiation attempt proved beyond doubt, Britain's diplomatic weight in Brussels is negligible. As one Council official frankly admitted: 'Even the best idea can die if it's presented by the UK.'[18]

In any case, the 'Missed Chances' thesis is based on a profound misreading of what actually happened during the 1950s. Britain was actively engaged in the debate, arguing for a loose free-trade area based on the seventeen OEEC members, and open to trade with other continents. It was the fact that she was making these arguments, rather than any sense of vanity or isolationism, that resulted in her exclusion.

At the Messina summit in 1955, a British official

18 *Daily Telegraph*, 15 December 2015

made a final, by then rather perfunctory, effort to push this idea – known in the foreign office as 'Plan G'. His arguments convinced the six foreign ministers of what was about to become the EEC that they needed to push ahead immediately, lest Britain's alternative plan gain traction.[19]

It is simply false to argue that, had Britain joined at the outset, the EU would have been a looser arrangement, based on free trade and national democracy. It was precisely because the six founding members did not want these things that they went ahead without the United Kingdom, signing the Treaty of Rome in 1957.

That did not end the discussions, though. The United Kingdom did not turn her back on the new bloc but continued to discuss the possibility of engagement, provided that the terms were economic rather than political. The Six were having none of it. For them, everything was about political union: they were not interested in any kind of loose, trade-based affiliation.

Britain continued to negotiate with the Six, applying for membership five years later under Harold Macmillan, and again seven years after that under Harold Wilson. Both times, the negotiations broke down over the issues that had precluded Britain's involvement in the first place: political union, the Common

19 Martin Schaad in *Contemporary European History*, 1998

Agricultural Policy and access for non-European, especially Commonwealth, imports.

In 1960, Britain took the lead in setting up a more comfortable bloc, the European Free Trade Association, along with Norway, Sweden, Denmark, Austria, Switzerland and Portugal. Unlike the EEC, EFTA had no interest in political amalgamation. Unlike the EEC, it was not a customs union but a free trade area.

This distinction might sound technical, but it is critical to our current referendum debate, so it's perhaps worth taking a moment to explain the difference. A free trade area is a group of states which have eliminated most or all tariffs and quotas on their trade. Sometimes, their agreement covers only manufactured goods and commodities. Sometimes it applies to services, too. In a few cases, it incorporates free movement of labour. Other examples of free trade areas, apart from EFTA, are NAFTA (Canada, the United States and Mexico) and ASEAN (ten South East Asian states).

A customs union, by contrast, involves internal free trade but also a common external tariff. Its members surrender their separate commercial policies and give up the right to sign trade agreements. Instead, trade negotiations are conducted, and treaties signed, by the bloc as a whole. Customs unions often exist where one state administers another, or where a tiny nation contracts out its trade policy to a larger neighbour: Swaziland and Lesotho are in a customs union with South Africa; Israel with the Palestinian territories. Other than the EU, the two chief customs unions on the planet are Mercosur and the Andean Community – both of which were created after heavy lobbying by the EU, which made clear that it would not sign worthwhile trade or aid deals with individual countries but would deal only bloc-to-bloc.

One way to think of the difference is this: NAFTA could accept Britain while allowing it to enjoy free trade with the EU; but the reverse is not true.

When Britain's second membership application was vetoed in 1967 by General de Gaulle, who cited her 'deep-seated hostility to European construction', it seemed a definitive settlement. Most observers assumed that there was now a stable and workable division in non-communist Europe between the six EEC members, committed to political unification, and the seven EFTA states, which wanted only unrestricted commerce. Commentators talked glibly of a Europe 'at Sixes and Sevens'.

It's true that, from the 1960s onwards, British diplomats began agitating for membership of the EEC. Quite how determinedly they manoeuvred towards accession was chronicled by the late Hugo Young in his 1998 book, *This Blessed Plot.*

Young was perhaps the most solidly Europhile writer of his day, and his book rehearses most of the usual arguments for the EU, notably that Britain is forever losing out by being stand-offish and joining too late. Yet he was also an exceptionally honest reporter, and was not too grand to roll up his sleeves and do some primary research. In particular, he tracked down many of the foreign office officials who had mounted Britain's three applications for membership. Now retired (usually to the south of France) these men spoke frankly about how they had, on occasion, acted directly contrary to the stated wishes of the government in order to pursue what they regarded as the national interest. Young, of course, regarded their attitude with approval but the general reader is left gasping. This is how he summarized what took place during the 1960s:

> An elite regiment was taking shape [in the FCO]. Europe wasn't yet the path of choice for every ambitious diplomat, but it promised to be much more interesting than the Commonwealth, and offered a prospect of influence greater than anything else available to a second-order power. By 1963, a corps of

diplomats was present in and around the Foreign Office who saw the future for both themselves and their country inside Europe. The interests of their country and their careers coincided. It was an appealing symbiosis.

Of course diplomats approve of the Brussels system: it was designed by diplomats for diplomats. But, throughout the 1960s, they kept running up against the reality that the terms being offered by the Six were unacceptable to British public opinion.

Then a freak occurrence changed everything. Edward Heath implausibly became leader of the Conservative Party and, in 1970, to everyone's astonishment, prime minister. Heath, who had been the chief negotiator during Macmillan's unsuccessful membership bid, was the most uncritical Euro-integrationist ever to have occupied a senior role in British politics. He was determined to get in on any terms, and the Six knew it.

It is hard to imagine any other politician being prepared to sacrifice so much in order to join. Heath acquiesced in full to the EU's agricultural and industrial policies, its external protectionism and its anti-Americanism. He not only accepted, but loudly applauded, its ambition to become a single state.

So abject was his attitude that, in the hours before joining, he handed away Britain's fishing grounds as a sort of late entry fee. Under maritime law, 65 per cent of the fish stocks in the EU's Channel and North Sea waters were in British territory. Under the Common Fisheries zto 25 per cent by volume or 15 per cent by value. The Norwegian fisheries minister resigned in protest when he learned what was being offered, and his country subsequently voted against accession in the referendum that Britain was denied until three years later.

Heath was even content to accept that the EU should carry on using its existing four official languages – French, German, Italian and Dutch. It was only at the insistence of Irish negotiators that English, too, was included.

It seems clear that Britain could have joined on such terms at any time. The metaphors about missing trains and boats and buses themselves all miss the point. To argue that the EU might have developed in a less federalist and less interventionist way had the United Kingdom been present from the start is to beg the question. Had Britain, or at least her leaders, remained opposed to federalism, she would never have joined. But, in the 1970s, worn down by what looked like permanent decline and industrial strife, and led by a man prepared to subordinate every other goal to accession, Britain seemed ready to go along with that enterprise.

Even so, the implications had to be hidden. Not even Heath tried to sell the project as being primarily about political merger – at least, not to his domestic audience. Instead, he appealed to the free-trading instincts of a merchant nation. The EEC was rechristened the 'Common Market' – and not only colloquially. In the 1975 referendum, the ballot paper referred explicitly to the Common Market, thereby implying that people were voting on a trade arrangement, not a political project.

Membership was advanced as a wholly economic proposition. Heath's nickname – the Grocer – came from his tendency to read out price lists, seeking to demonstrate that essential household goods were cheaper on the Continent than in Britain. The implications for sovereignty were not simply minimized, they were expressly denied. In a television broadcast to mark Britain's formal accession to the EEC in 1973, the prime minister declared: 'There are some in this country who fear that in going into Europe we shall in some way sacrifice independence and sovereignty. These fears, I need hardly say, are completely unjustified.'[20]

That statement has been thrown back at the

20 BBC broadcast, 2 January 1973

Conservative Party ever since. People felt, with reason, that they had been deceived by their leaders, that they had joined on a false premise. Instead of becoming members of what they had assumed to be a free market, based on the unrestricted circulation of goods and mutual recognition of products, they had joined a quasi-state which was in the process of acquiring all the machinery of democratic representation and legal coercive power.

At the same time, the common market itself never properly materialized. As we have seen, the European Commission was keener on standardization than on mutual product recognition. Rather than ruling that if, say, a bottle of mineral water was legal in Britain, it might also be legally sold in Italy, and vice versa, the EU tended to lay down precise specifications: that the bottle should have a volume of not less than X and not more than Y, that certain minerals had to be included and certain others excluded and so on. Manufacturers and retailers who had no export trade – and the majority of firms do business only locally – might nonetheless find their product prohibited. Instead of expanding consumer choice, the European authorities were restricting it.

We can say with some certainty that the costs of regulation in the EU outweigh the benefits of the single market. The reason we can be sure is that we have the figures from the European Commission itself. The Commission tells us that the single market boosts the EU's GDP by 120 billion euros a year. We might cavil at this figure, of course. The Commission is hardly a disinterested assessor; it has every reason to talk up the numbers. Nonetheless, let us be generous and allow, for the sake of argument, that that figure is accurate. In November 2004, the then internal market commissioner, Guenther Verheugen, asked his department to assess the total cost of business regulation in the EU. The answer? Six hundred billion euros a year. Thus, by the Commission's own admission, the economic costs of the EU then outweighed the benefits fivefold.[21] And that was before the euro crisis had begun.

Britain was not the only state to have joined for largely economic reasons. Ireland and Denmark joined on the same day, largely as a consequence of British accession. Sweden, too, saw membership as being essentially about market access. In all of these countries, the mood turned as the promised benefits failed to materialize.

It was Britain, though, where the reaction was strongest. This was partly because the cost–benefit analysis was more clearly negative for the UK than

21 *EU Competitiveness Report*, 5 November 2004

for any other state. Britain has paid more into the EU budget than she has received back in forty-one out of forty-two years of membership (the exception, tellingly, being 1975: the year of the referendum on withdrawal). Indeed, for most of those forty-two years, there were only two net contributors: Britain and Germany.

Britain was doubly penalized by the Common Agricultural Policy: as a net food importer with an efficient farming sector, she was hit both positively and negatively, paying more in and getting less back.

She was, of course, uniquely deleteriously impacted by the Common Fisheries Policy which, for the next thirty years, did not apply to the Mediterranean or the Baltic, but only to the North Sea. It was, in other words, an overtly anti-British policy.

And, as we have seen, her trade suffered as the Common External Tariff wrenched her away from her traditional commercial partners. Britain had run a trade surplus with the Six prior to membership. In 1973, that trade went into deficit, where it has remained to this day. Indeed, over the forty-two years of her membership of the EU, Britain has run a cumulative trade surplus with every continent in the world except Europe. She has had to make up, through her exports to North America, South America, Africa, Asia and Australia, the current account deficit she runs with the EU.

Fig. 7

WHAT GOES UP AND
NEVER COMES DOWN?

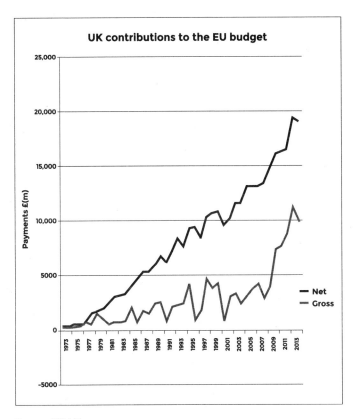

Source: HM Treasury

Britain finds herself isolated in the EU, not because of any conspiracy against her but because she differs from the others politically and economically. In a union where decisions are made by majority, and may be imposed on dissenters, members will suffer to the extent that they diverge from the mean. No country diverges as much as Britain.

The divergence, as we have seen in this chapter, is partly economic, and partly political. As Denman, the civil servant who steered us in, lamented near the end of his life, 'We are happy with a trading arrangement, a common market. But we will not count until we make a political commitment. We have never faced up to the fact that we would have to trade power for power.'

There being no sign that the British people are any readier to become patriotic citizens of Europe, that isolation will continue. Britain will carry on being outvoted and ignored. The precious 'influence' which EU supporters keep conjuring will remain a wholly notional concept, one that we are somehow never able to exercise. Influence, in the mind of the British Eurocrat, can only ever be stored, never spent. The moment the United Kingdom asserts herself, the talk of 'influence' is replaced by talk of 'intransigence'.

But it is not only Britain's history and geography that set her apart, not only her ties of kinship and migration to other Anglophone states, not only her service-based, open, deep-water economy. Perhaps the single biggest obstacle in the path of her integration with the EU is a difference in how her citizens relate to her government – a difference rooted in the twin concepts of common law and parliamentary supremacy.

6

SOVEREIGNTY OF
THE PEOPLE

IF YOU WERE elected to the European Parliament having previously served as an MP in a Continental country, the chances are you would feel quite at home. The chamber would remind you of your national legislature, with representatives sitting behind desks in a broad semi-circle, and the parties ranged from Left to Right politically: the Communists to the president's far left, then the Greens, then the Socialists, then the Liberals and so on. As in most Continental assemblies, proportional voting at European elections ensures representation for several parties.

The European Parliament is a relatively weak body. It cannot, except in very special circumstances, propose laws. Rather, its role is to amend legislation put before it by the unelected European Commission – a division of powers which, again, is not so different from what happens in several legislatures on the Continent, but would be unthinkable in Britain. MEPs favour consensus and like to bring as many parties as possible into their majority coalitions. Their main work is technical, and such politics as takes place happens in committees, not on the floor of the chamber.

Speeches to plenary sessions are necessarily perfunctory affairs, since most MEPs get no more than two or three minutes to make them. This doesn't allow them any time to respond to earlier interventions or to develop arguments. To a British legislator, brought up to think of parliamentary debates as things of moment, it all seems rather alien. But to, say, a Spaniard, it feels familiar enough.

These differences, though, are just symptoms – expressions of a much deeper divergence in constitutional arrangements. In twenty-seven of the twenty-eight EU states, a written constitution is supreme and parliament is subordinate. The United Kingdom, as so often, is the exception.

The Continental model can be translated easily enough to EU level. For most member states, the difference between Brussels and their national institutions is one of location rather than of quality. Supreme power in the EU is vested, at least in theory, in a written constitution. True, it's not called a constitution but that is a technical detail.

The EU's constitution was drafted in 2004 and put to the member states for ratification in the form of the Treaty Establishing a Constitution for Europe. When that treaty was rejected in referendums in France and the Netherlands in 2005, Eurocrats decided to keep the contents but change the name. Why? Because a new name was politically necessary to allow several national governments, including Britain's, to wriggle out of their promises to hold a referendum on the text. As the author of the European Constitution, Valéry Giscard d'Estaing, frankly admitted: 'The institutional proposals of the constitutional treaty are found complete in the Lisbon Treaty, only in a different order.'[22]

So, the EU has a written constitution, cited in the same reverential tone as any national constitution. Eurocrats like to describe themselves, slightly portentously, as 'guardians of the treaties'. Those treaties are interpreted (just as, in twenty-seven of the twenty-eight member states, the national constitution is interpreted) by a supreme court.

22 *Le Monde*, 26 October 2007

Curiously, the EU's supreme court is called the European Court of Justice (ECJ), though it has always functioned as a constitutional tribunal rather than a criminal court. As with all supreme courts, it can be prone to judicial activism – that is, to ruling on the basis of what it thinks the law ought to say rather than what it says. Again, this is more shocking to British than Continental sensibilities. Judicial activism is arguably inevitable when you have a supreme court – though, in fairness, few national supreme courts can match the ECJ when it comes to the sheer flagrancy of its creative interpretation.

One example may stand for many. When the EU wanted to extend its jurisdiction into social policy and employment law, it needed the permission of all member states. The UK opposed the move but eventually agreed to allow the others to go ahead, using the institutions of the EU, provided there was a legal guarantee that Britain would not be forced to join in. The moment the ink was dry on that guarantee, the then eleven other states began to agitate to extend their rules to the UK. Because Britain had an opt-out on social and employment policy, they reintroduced the main pillar of that policy – a directive regulating paid holidays, maximum weekly working times and the like – as a 'health and safety' measure (the 1993 Working Time Directive).

The Major government protested that the measure was plainly social policy rather than health and safety – it allowed employees to work more than forty-eight hours a week, provided they were given overtime – but the ECJ decided that health and safety didn't just mean being safe at work: it also meant looking after the 'social well-being' of employees.

The point is not whether the Working Time Directive is a good or a bad idea. The point is that the ECJ was behaving as a legislative rather than a judicial body, disregarding the plain meaning of the law in pursuit of a political objective. It has since then, incidentally, repeatedly extended the scope of the Working Time Directive, most recently ruling, in 2015, that the time spent travelling to and from your place of work must count towards your forty-eight hours. Again, whatever the rights and wrongs of that ruling, it is surely a decision for elected governments to make.

Tendentious rulings of this kind – the ECJ recently managed to offend not 50 per cent but 100 per cent of the population, first ruling that women might not be offered cheaper car insurance and then ruling that men might not be offered cheaper annuities – are always more controversial in Britain than on the Continent. My MEP colleagues from other countries often put this down to Britain having a more Eurosceptic culture, but I'd put it the other way around. Britain's organic, bottom-up, anti-authoritarian traditions are the origin of her Euroscepticism, not a product of it.

As well as a powerful supreme court, the EU has a powerful civil service. Indeed, there is no real distinction in Brussels between the civil service and the cabinet: the European Commission combines both roles, being generally staffed by doctrinaire former politicians who are appointed rather than elected. Yet again, this has always been more of an issue on this side of the Channel. As we saw in Chapter Three, British Eurosceptics have complained since the 1960s about 'unelected European commissioners'. Although this line of criticism is echoed in some other member states, notably in Scandinavia, many Europeans regard unelected ministers as quite normal and have never understood what the fuss is about.

The EU, not unreasonably, reflects the majority practice of its member states in its own structures. This does not imply any kind of conspiracy against Britain. It's simply that Britain has a very different constitutional framework, and therefore finds herself having to adjust more than any other state in order to conform.

What is the root of British constitutional particularism? It has to do, above all, with the role of Parliament.

Almost exactly 800 years ago, in a meadow by a reedy stretch of the River Thames in my constituency, a bargain was struck which established the principle that the king could no longer make up the law as he went along. It was a moment of planetary significance: the first time, anywhere, that the concept of the rule of law took written, contractual form. But what made Magna Carta truly exceptional is that it contained its own enforcement mechanism – a form of conciliar government that was to develop, over the next fifty years, into a bicameral assembly meeting at Westminster.

In the English, and later British, tradition, Parliament was the supreme expression and the ultimate defence of the rule of law. Constitutional government was not guaranteed by an independent panel that stood apart from the legislature. It was up to Parliament, and therefore to the people who elected Parliament, to safeguard their own freedoms.

In much Continental political theory, there is a tension between liberty and democracy. A majority, goes the argument, might oppress a minority. There is therefore a continuing debate about where to draw the line between constitutional freedom and majority rule. But in the Westminster tradition, Parliament's first duty is not to represent public opinion but to hold the government in check.

It is worth noting as an aside that, although the Continental model of a written constitution and guaranteed rights is attractive in theory, it hasn't always worked in practice. If voters contract out their essential freedoms to a constitutional court, they have no fall-back should that court fail or be subverted. If you read the constitution of, say East Germany, you'll find ringing guarantees of freedom of conscience, assembly and speech. But, as the citizens of that unhappy state knew, paper rights are worthless without mechanisms of representative government to hold rulers to account.

One way of putting it is that the British tradition is more concerned with the practice than the theory of freedom, impatient with sonorous declarations and charters. As a young Benjamin Disraeli told the solid country folk of his constituency: 'I prefer the liberties we enjoy to the liberalism they profess, and find something better than the Rights of Man in the rights of Englishmen.'

Britain is unusual in another regard, too. Its legal system – or at least that of England, Wales and Northern Ireland – is based on common law rather than civil law. While around a third of the world's population operates under some form of common law, most of the EU works with Roman-based civil law.

Only Cyprus and the Republic of Ireland are in company with Britain.

The difference between the two systems is worth exploring. Most legal systems are top-down: a law is written down in the abstract and then applied to particular disputes as they arise. But the common law, bizarrely, was never planned. It grew from beneath like a coral, each judgment serving as the starting-point for the next case. How did it begin? No one really knows. And, in theory, you might not expect it to work as well as a rational civil law system does. Yet, in practice, there has been no surer guarantee of freedom. As John Adams, the second president of the United States, put it, 'The liberty, the unalienable, indefeasible rights of men, the honour and dignity of human nature... and the universal happiness of individuals, were never so skilfully and successfully consulted as in that most excellent monument of human art, the common law of England.'

Because the common law comes from the people rather than the state, it developed in opposition to state power. It assumes residual freedoms: that which is not explicitly prohibited is implicitly allowed. This perhaps partly explains the difference in political attitudes that I see every week in the European Parliament. Faced with a proposal for some new regulatory power, or some new EU directive, the first instinct of a British MEP is to ask: 'What problem would this solve? Why do we need it?'

To which the usual answer is: 'But the existing system is unregulated!' The idea that lack of regulation might be a natural condition, that you shouldn't need a licence from the government before embarking on a new venture, is regarded as an Anglo-Saxon eccentricity. In the mind of a Eurocrat, 'unregulated' and 'illegal' are almost synonymous concepts.

Britain's legal system, like her political system, is organic rather than prescriptive. It was a product of unplanned evolution rather than conscious design. I'm not arguing that this makes us better people: every country has its own traditions and its own peculiarities. I'm simply trying to explain why it is that, in an EU that is the ultimate expression of top-down planning, or bureaucratic fiat, Britain tends to feel more uncomfortable than other nations.

Britain is in a small minority, globally, in having no written constitution. And, for what it's worth, I am prepared to listen to the arguments for having one. Be that as it may, though, Britain's status as the only one of twenty-eight EU members without a written constitution leaves her in an exceptionally vulnerable position vis-à-vis the Brussels institutions. To explain why, we need to consider what makes the EU different from all other international organizations.

Pro-EU campaigners like to talk about the importance of 'co-operation', implying that those who want to leave the EU are somehow against working with our neighbours. But if co-operation were all that were involved, if the EU were simply an international club like NATO or the Commonwealth, there would be little argument over our membership and we wouldn't now be holding this referendum.

What makes the EU Treaties unique is that they don't simply bind their signatories as states; they create a new legal order, which members must accept as superior to their own, and which is directly enforced by the national courts, even when the national parliament says otherwise.

It is worth emphasizing how this works. Suppose Parliament were to pass a law limiting net inward migration from other EU countries to 100,000 people a year. The moment the 100,001st EU citizen was denied residence, he would be able to challenge his deportation before a British court. That court, obedient to the 1972 European Communities Act, which instructs the Bench to give precedence to EU decisions over British statutes, would automatically uphold his right to remain in Britain and, indeed, to claim benefits in line with the provisions of the European Treaties. There would be no need for the European Commission to take Britain to court: our own judges would do its work for it.

Curiously enough, the supremacy of EU law wasn't written into the Treaty of Rome. It was never agreed to by the member governments. Rather, it was a doctrine invented by the European Court of Justice, in a series of controversial judgments in the 1960s that even committed Euro-federalists now admit amounted to a judicial *coup d'état*. First, Euro-judges declared that their decisions were directly binding upon individuals and businesses in the member states, then that they had precedence even over national constitutions – a doctrine still rejected in theory by most of the national supreme courts.

In the United Kingdom, the supremacy of EU law was confirmed by what is known as the Factortame case, which saw the 1988 Merchant Shipping Act disapplied by our domestic courts because it was held to be at odds with EU rulings. The case concerned the right of foreign vessels to fish against the UK's quota under the Common Fisheries Policy – which, you will recall, is a far smaller quota than would be the case if the UK simply controlled her own territorial waters, out to 200 nautical miles or the median line, as allowed under maritime law. Ever since Britain joined the EEC, some foreign vessels had been registering as British in order to land fish that were within the UK share, a process that accelerated when Spain joined in 1986.

The 1988 Merchant Shipping Act sought to tighten the rules on registration by specifying that, in order to qualify as British, a vessel must have a majority British crew or some other qualifying connection to the UK. 'Factortame' was the name of one of the Spanish-owned companies: firms that must register for purely procedural reasons often make use of invented names of this sort. Its lawyers challenged the legislation on grounds that it contradicted the essential principles of the Common Fisheries Policy, which define fish stocks as a 'common resource' to which all member states have 'equal access'.

There is not space in this book to recount the entire legal proceedings, the various appeals, the ping-pong between British courts, the ECJ and the House of Lords. To cut a long story short, the 1988 legislation was set aside by our own courts, supported by the ECJ. Even an explicit Act of Parliament was deemed inferior to EU rules. That is what loss of sovereignty means in practice.

7

EUROPE – YOUR COUNTRY

SUPPOSE – AND YOU MIGHT NOT find this easy – that you really wanted the EU to be a superstate. We keep being assured by pro-EU politicians, at least in Britain, that nobody is proposing such a thing. So, just as an intellectual exercise, imagine that you really did support it. What would you want the EU to do that it isn't already doing?

To ask the question is to see how many of the attributes of statehood the EU has already acquired. Statehood is defined, in international law, by Article One of the 1933 Montevideo Convention on the Rights and Duties of States:

> The state as a person of international law should possess the following qualifications: (a) a permanent population; (b) a defined territory; (c) government; and (d) capacity to enter into relations with the other states.

Well, the EU certainly possesses (a). There are 507 million EU nationals who have, since 1993, possessed a common citizenship. That citizenship is not simply decorative. It bestows enforceable legal rights, including the ability to work and settle in any EU state and to vote in other countries' elections. It prohibits 'discrimination on grounds of nationality' – an entitlement that has been interpreted almost open-endedly by the ECJ to break down national sovereignty. Indeed, the Court made its views plain in a ruling in 1999: 'EU Citizenship is destined to be the fundamental status of nationals of the Member States.'[23] In other words, while we might keep elements of our old nationalities too, it'll be primarily as EU citizens that we engage politically.

How about (b), 'a defined territory'? Since the mid-1990s, the EU has been gradually dismantling what it calls its 'internal' borders – that is, the frontiers

23 *Rudy Grzelczyk* v *Centre public d'aide sociale d'Ottignies-Louvain-la-Neuve*

between its member states – and replacing them with an 'external' border, policed by an EU agency called Frontex. The 2015 migration crisis put both aspects of this policy under strain. The 'external' border turned out to be very permeable indeed. In fact, it soon became clear that the dismantling of the 'internal' borders had exacerbated its permeability, because it encouraged some of the EU's more southerly and easterly members to wave illicit migrants through, knowing that they would become someone else's responsibility. At the end of 2015, in desperation, several EU states began unilaterally to reimpose border controls. Nonetheless, by any measure, the EU has a defined territory.

Government? Check. The EU has a parliament, a supreme court, a central bank, a civil service and, since 2009, a president – first the Belgian politician Herman Van Rompuy, now the former Polish prime minister, Donald Tusk. It carries out all the definitive functions of government, from taxation to policing. Of course, it doesn't have a monopoly on these things: taxation and policing have local, national and European dimensions. Nonetheless, the machinery of state in Brussels – 23,000 officials at the European Commission, 6,000 at the European Parliament and many more at the associated agencies – surely constitutes a government.

Which leaves only (d): 'capacity to enter into relations with other states'. This was the last to come. Only with the entry into force of the Lisbon Treaty at the end of 2009 did the EU acquire the panoply of diplomatic representation: a foreign minister, a diplomatic corps (the European External Action Service), embassies and, crucially, legal personality and treaty-making powers. In 2010, the EU secured what many regard as the ultimate test of statehood, namely the right to be represented at the United Nations. It was to have the same prerogatives as any nation – 'the right to speak in a timely manner, the right of reply, the right to circulate documents, the right to make proposals and submit amendments, the right to raise points of order'.

Taken together, I'd say that amounts to being something very like a state, whether or not you favour the neologism 'superstate'. Certainly it is far more than a club of nations or an international association like the IMF, OPEC or ASEAN.

One measure of the EU's quasi-national status is that it has acquired the symbolic trappings of nationhood: a flag (twelve gold stars on a blue background); a national anthem (Beethoven's Ninth Symphony, to which we're expected to stand to attention in Brussels, though I find it's starting to have the same effect on me as on Alex in Anthony Burgess's 1962 novel

A Clockwork Orange – and for the same reason, namely bad connotations); national holiday (9 May – Europe Day); a driving licence; a passport. As the sign in the European Commission building in Brussels puts it: 'Europe – your country'.

Curiously, those in Brussels who are loudest in their denunciations of nationalism often turn out to be all for it as soon as the symbols are switched to a European level. To talk of asserting the national interests of Britain or Sweden is considered boorish. But to talk of Europe needing to come together so as to assert itself against the United States and China is seen as sensible statecraft.

So, let's return to the question. If you wanted the EU to be a superstate, what would you change? The answer, as far as institutions go, is surely 'not much'. Perhaps you'd like the European Parliament to have more power, the EU budget to be larger, and the various fiscal transfer mechanisms to be rationalized into a proper EU taxation system. No doubt you'd want to give Brussels more direct control over criminal justice, energy policy, defence and the like. But the basic structures are already in place. You wouldn't need to make any revolutionary changes; you could afford to sit back and let the existing bureaucracies enlarge their powers – as all bureaucracies do.

In fact, this is, broadly speaking, what supporters of a United States of Europe have been doing since the rejection of the European Constitution by the French and Dutch electorates in 2005. That was the last time they placed their scheme fully and plainly before the voters – not a mistake they'll make again in a hurry.

I well remember how my colleagues' mood changed after those votes. Until then, like so many people living in bubbles, Eurocrats and MEPs had come to believe their own propaganda. Surrounded by EU-funded think-tanks and pressure groups, attending EU-funded seminars and colloquiums, they had truly convinced themselves that most people shared their enthusiasm for federalism. True, there might be one or two hold-outs, such as Britain with its Eurosceptic press barons; but, even there, voters would surely come round to the idea of a united Europe in due course.

The two referendum defeats, coming within days of each other, were a massive psychological trauma for Europhiles. Many simply denied the results, insisting that the referendums had been about something else. Surely the French had really been voting against Jacques Chirac, or Turkish accession, or Anglo-Saxon liberalism – against anything, in fact, except the proposition actually on the ballot paper. Others acknowledged the verdict intellectually but could not accept it emotionally. I remember a French friend, a senior Commission official, asking in wonder: 'How can my countrymen have drifted so far away from me?' (It is human nature, I suppose, to place yourself at the centre of the universe.)

Since then, the European project has returned to what is known as the Monnet Method. The EU's canny founder, Jean Monnet, was the ultimate networker. He understood that politicians came and went but bureaucracies were permanent. The key to success, therefore, was to stack the incentives in such a way as to encourage officials to pursue an integrationist agenda. Some political scientists call this process 'functionalism' – although, as so often, that word has many different academic meanings.

Call it what we will, this method was how the EU advanced between the 1950s and the early 1980s. The phase when federalists argued openly and proudly for their vision lasted, broadly speaking, from the Jacques Delors years in the late 1980s until the French and Dutch referendums in 2005. After that, the EU went back to its roots: to closed summits and back-room deals, to judiciously targeted financial grants and job offers.

Deeper integration is pursued not through open debates and referendums, but through Commission

decisions, ECJ rulings, creative extensions of jurisdiction and, above all, through the deft exploitation
of crises. There's a debt problem? We need European
taxes! There's a migration problem? We need a common
asylum policy! The agenda is swaddled in bureaucratic
language, and presented as an issue-by-issue response
to practical challenges. Very rarely nowadays do federalists admit that they would be pursuing these goals
anyway in order to give the EU the characteristics
of nationhood.

All the institutions are in place; and all except the
euro apply to the United Kingdom. Britain is subject
to the jurisdiction of the ECJ and the rulings of the
Brussels institutions. Her people are EU citizens. She
participates in all the main common policies: trade,
agriculture, foreign affairs, culture and so on. Even her
opt-out from monetary union is a lot less significant
than you might think. True, there is no way that
Britain can be forced to surrender the pound. But she
has been, and is being, dragged into all the policies
that have been raised as scaffolding around the euro,
the policies needed to hold it in place, including the
European Central Bank, the bailouts, the budget
monitoring and the fiscal transfers.

The right to mint your own currency is not, in itself,
a guarantee of independence if you surrender the other

tools of economic sovereignty. Scotland and Northern Ireland print their own pound notes but in neither case does this mean that they are sovereign entities. The EU is accelerating its push to political union in order to preserve the euro. The single currency, all now agree, cannot be held together without some form of fiscal union – that is, automatic transfers of wealth from the richer to the poorer areas. Fiscal union implies political union, because no one will agree to create such a structure without democratic oversight. And, as the Five Presidents' Report makes clear, that political union will be pursued within the context of the EU as a whole, not just of the eurozone. Britain, in other words, will be part of it, pound or no pound.

It is important to understand that this agenda is not a response to the euro crisis. Rather, the euro crisis is just the latest event that has been conscripted as an argument in favour of the agenda that is being pursued regardless. The Brussels institutions never renounced their foundational ideology. In his first speech to the European Parliament as president of the European Commission in 2014, Jean-Claude Juncker praised Jacques Delors as his 'hero and inspiration' and went on to call for the harmonization of social security, the creation of a pan-European minimum wage and the consolidation of an EU army. The speech was unusual, not because any of these proposals is considered *outré* in Brussels, but because most Eurocrats have learned, since 2005, not to talk about them in public.

How do I know that they say these things in private? Well, for one thing, I know because I work in Brussels and Strasbourg, so I hear such sentiments every day. But don't take my word for it. In Appendix One, I have compiled some of the things that senior EU leaders have said on the record. Run your eye over it and then try to tell me that the enthusiasm for a United States of Europe is waning.

Let's very slightly rephrase the question with which I opened the chapter. If you were a British Euroenthusiast, committed to ensuring that your country remained part of the continuing political integration of the EU, if you disliked the idea of any kind of special status or associate membership almost as much as the idea of withdrawal, what would be your wisest course?

Again, surely the answer is obvious. All you would need to do is ensure that the country remained a member of the EU. Everything else would follow as the institutions did their work.

Of course, in order to keep the country in the EU, you wouldn't talk openly about political union, any more than Edward Heath did in the early 1970s.

In fact, you'd do precisely as he did: you'd try to frame the argument wholly in economic terms. If necessary, you'd deny the political goal – what Eurocrats call the *finalité politique* – outright. You'd insist that non-membership of the euro amounted to some kind of 'special status' for Britain. You'd say that we were no longer bound by the goal of ever-closer union.

Which is more or less what the prime minister has been doing. 'We are a proud and independent nation – with proud, independent, democratic institutions that have served us well over the centuries,' he told MPs on returning with the arrangement he had agreed with the European Commission, the so-called 'renegotiation'.

'For us, Europe is about working together to advance our shared prosperity and our shared security. It is not about being sucked into some kind of European superstate. Not now. Not ever.'

Let's explore that claim.

8

FRIED AIR

THE BRITISH, RUNS the Brussels cliché, have always wanted it both ways on the EU. They want the trade, but they don't want the political union. 'You can't be half-in and half-out,' say Eurocrats; an assertion dutifully echoed by their allies and auxiliaries in London.

The line is usually delivered with Olympian certainty, as if the speaker were citing some law of physics. In fact, if you think about it, there is no reason why a country shouldn't be half-in and half-out, participating in some common policy areas but not in others. Indeed, that description applies to virtually every non-EU territory in Europe, from Iceland and the Channel Islands to Switzerland and Turkey. The only question is whether a state can enjoy such a status while being a member of the EU.

There is little doubt that most British voters want to be half-in and half-out. At the time of writing, the opinion polls are evenly balanced on the question of whether to leave the EU. But as soon as you throw in a third option – a looser deal, where we are in the common market but outside the common political structures – approval shoots up to 70 per cent or more.

Which is why David Cameron decided to precede the referendum with a renegotiation, aimed at establishing some new status along those lines. It is worth retelling the story of that renegotiation, because there can be no clearer demonstration of quite how intractable the EU is – and, frankly, of quite how disdainful its leaders are towards Britain's wishes.

Supporters of continued membership like to assert that no renegotiation would have satisfied Eurosceptics but this is demonstrably untrue. I know of almost no one who sees leaving the EU as an end in itself. People who want Brexit see it, rather, as a means to an end – that end being a more prosperous, more democratic and freer United Kingdom. Obviously, if that end could be achieved through a renegotiation, we'd back it.

I have been able to dig out eleven of my own articles written between the announcement that there would be a referendum in January 2013 and the conclusion of the negotiations in February 2016 setting out what I thought would constitute a satisfactory deal. Other Eurosceptic politicians and columnists were also engaged in setting out their agendas. In the end, we agreed on three core aims: the primacy of UK over EU law on our own territory; the right to sign bilateral trade deals with non-EU states, such as Australia and India; and the right to control who can settle in the UK. None of these aims is in any sense immoderate or unreasonable. That they evidently cannot be reconciled with EU membership tells us a great deal about the nature of the EU.

In the event, David Cameron did not pursue either of our first two aims. The third – border control – was something that he did not mention when he began the renegotiation process, although he added it when it became clear that his other declared objectives couldn't be met. In the event, he must regret ever having raised the hope of any significant tightening of our immigration policy.

So, what did the prime minister ask for? Initially, he set out a broad but shallow reform package. While most of the changes he sought were modest – docile, we might almost say – they did at least cover a wide range of areas. And yet, unassuming as they were, they encountered opposition during the exploratory talks, and so were dropped from the list.

It is worth noting the promises that never made it past this first stage – the things, in other words, that David Cameron had publicly demanded in the run-up to the talks, but which had to be abandoned before he formally put his requests in writing. To list them is to see how much had to be given away before the formal process even began.

'To restore social and employment legislation to national control.'[24]

'A complete opt-out from the Charter of Fundamental Rights.'[25]

'Limiting the European Court of Justice's jurisdiction over criminal law to its pre-Lisbon level.'[26]

'We want EU jobseekers to have a job offer before they come here.'[27]

'If an EU jobseeker has not found work within six months, they will be required to leave.'

'Revising the Working Time Directive at EU level to give the NHS the flexibility it needs.'[28]

24 *Guardian*, 6 March 2007
25 Speech, 4 November 2009
26 Speech, 4 November 2009
27 Speech, 28 November 2014
28 Hansard, col 746, 18 January 2012

'The European Parliament must end its absurdly wasteful habit of meeting in Strasbourg as well as in Brussels.'[29]

'Reform of the EU's Common Agricultural Policy.'[30]

'Reform of EU Structural Funds.'[31]

'Treaty change that I'll be putting in place before the referendum.'[32]

This last point is critical. The EU Treaties are, as we have seen, the EU's constitution, its supreme authority. If a national government, or a group of national governments – or even, in theory, all twenty-eight national governments – act in a way that is not in line with the treaties, their actions will be struck down. It was precisely to secure a treaty change that the prime minister originally proposed a delay before the vote.

When he first announced a referendum on leaving the EU, in a speech at Bloomberg in January 2013, he expected – as did almost everyone else, to be fair – that the EU would soon have to draw up a new treaty in order to regularize the euro bailouts which, at that time, were patently illegal. He therefore announced that the referendum would take place by the end of 2017, so

29 Conservative European election manifesto, 2014
30 Conservative general election manifesto, 2015
31 Conservative general election manifesto, 2015
32 *Daily Telegraph*, 5 January 2014

as to allow time for the new treaty to be negotiated and for his multiple if minor aims to be incorporated into it.

As late as 2015, David Cameron was still insisting that 'proper, full-on treaty change' was a necessary part of the deal.[33] But he underestimated the EU's readiness to maintain an essentially illegal situation over the bailouts. The other member states and, even more, the Brussels institutions, had internalized the lessons of the 2005 French and Dutch votes against the European Constitution. They did not want to push through a new treaty and thereby trigger more referendums. Better by far to use the Monnet Method: to advance in the shadows, on the edge of legality, by bureaucratic fiat.

So David Cameron found himself in the uncomfortable position of asking for changes that could not be delivered. Without a new treaty, as all sides were aware, there would be no binding changes. Britain was reduced to getting a declaration from the other heads of government to the effect that a few things might be looked at or reconsidered.

Indeed, far from preparing a new treaty, the president of the European Council, Donald Tusk, used the process explicitly to reaffirm the authority of the existing treaties. The opening line of his summary of the deal with David Cameron asserted that everything

33 *The Andrew Marr Show*, BBC1, 4 January 2015

which followed was 'in conformity with the Treaties'. In other words, nothing might be interpreted as a change to the pre-existing rules. Just in case anyone missed the point, his summary spelt it out: 'The competences conferred by the Member States on the Union can be modified, whether to increase or reduce them, only through a revision of the Treaties with the agreement of all Member States.' And there is no revision of the treaties; there is, indeed, a proposal to modify just one directive on access to welfare – something which could have been agreed without any renegotiations and which could, of course, be undone at any time.

As the president of the European Parliament, Martin Schulz, put it on a visit to London three days after Donald Tusk had summarized his talking points: 'Nothing is irreversible.'[34]

If, indeed, things were to get even that far. Shortly after the February summit at which the 'deal' was agreed, it emerged that Angela Merkel had told fellow EU leaders: 'On the question of amending the Treaties, we do not know if we ever will have to change them.'[35] François Hollande went further and in public: 'No revision of the Treaties is planned.'[36]

34 Sky News, 5 February 2016
35 *Independent on Sunday*, 21 February 2016
36 *Journal de Dimanche*, 21 February 2016

In other words, nothing fundamental is even notion-ally being changed. The legality of the status quo is expressly reaffirmed. All that is being discussed is a political agreement to look at some of the rules inside the existing framework. And even this agreement might be reversed.

In fact, though, there is nothing of substance to reverse. Having dropped the ten pledges listed above, David Cameron went into the talks with just four remaining objectives: boosting competitiveness; protec-ting the position of non-euro states; strengthening national parliaments; and limiting migration.

The first two aims were never intended to be any-thing other than declaratory. 'More competitiveness' is one of those platitudes that every Brussels official and every national politician has been trotting out for decades. When I was a new MEP in 2000, the Union had just adopted something called the 'Lisbon Agenda', designed to give it, by 2010, 'the most com-petitive and dynamic knowledge-based economy in the world capable of sustainable economic growth with more and better jobs and greater social cohesion'. When 2010 came, of course, the EU was in recession, unemployment was rising and every other region in the world had comprehensively outperformed the EU, whose growth rate, during the first decade of the twenty-first century, was just one-third of the global average. So what lesson did EU leaders draw from this abject failure? They decided to repeat precisely the same exercise, promptly adopting the 'Europe 2020' strategy, aimed at producing 'smart, sustainable, inclusive growth'. The words mean no more than the slogans that accompanied Five Year Plans in the Soviet Union. Now the prime minister has won an additional platitude, to the effect that the EU will 'make all efforts to strengthen the internal market'. No one – literally no one – expects it to make any difference.

This is true, too, of the second stated commitment, namely 'protecting the status of non-euro states'. This ambition was originally understood to mean that, on issues of key economic importance, the voting weights would be adjusted so that measures could not be imposed on non-euro countries by the votes of the eurozone alone. The UK had lost several court cases over EU regulations and directives that seemed deliberately and maliciously targeted at London, by far the EU's largest financial centre. In the event, though, 'protecting the status of the non-euro states' was redefined as stating that they were under no obligation to join the euro – in Britain's case, a statement of the obvious. It emphatically doesn't mean that Britain won't end up being drawn into measures adopted by the EU to keep the single currency together. The prime minister asserted on securing the statement that Britain would be exempted from having to bail out the euro – which seems somewhat forgetful since, in the same speech at Bloomberg in which he had launched the renegotiation three years earlier, he had declared: 'Look at what we have achieved already. Ending Britain's obligation to bail out eurozone members.' That achievement, of which he went on to boast throughout the general election, even putting it in the May 2015 manifesto, was shown to be nonsense in June 2015, when Britain was dragged, against her will, into the third Greek bailout.

The third commitment, the strengthening of national parliaments, has led to a proposal which is arguably worse than the status quo. Unable to secure the right of a national parliament to override EU rules, British negotiators eventually came back with something called the 'red card' proposal, which gives the national parliaments of the EU a theoretical right to block a Commission proposal if 55 per cent of them simultaneously demand it. The right is, however, wholly notional. An existing 'yellow card' mechanism, which needs only 35 per cent of parliaments to be triggered – not 55 per cent – has been used only twice during the six years of its existence, and on one of those occasions it was ignored. No one seriously imagines that more than half the national parliaments could all be brought to vote against the same proposal at the same moment – a point made very ably by none other than William Hague, responding in the House of Commons to an identical proposal in 2008, with George Osborne and David Cameron roaring with laughter alongside him:

> Given the difficulty of Oppositions winning a vote in their Parliaments, the odds against doing so in fourteen countries around Europe with different parliamentary recesses are such that even if the European Commission proposed the slaughter of the first-born it would be difficult to achieve such a remarkable conjunction of parliamentary votes.

But the measure isn't useless, it is actively harmful. For the first time in its 750-year history, Parliament is formally recognized as a sub-unit within a larger polity. The 'red card' initiative treats the EU's national parliaments like state legislatures in the US – which are empowered to make constitutional amendments if they club together in the right proportion. Instead of being a sovereign entity in voluntary association with others, Parliament implicitly accepts a subordinate status. And all in exchange for a blocking power that will never in fact be exercised.

Which leaves the fourth objective, and the one that attracted the most media interest in the UK, namely the idea of restricting migration from the EU. Again, it is interesting to see how the same words were used, with what can only be deliberate obfuscation, to hide the retreat from one position to another.

What the prime minister originally wanted was an 'emergency brake' on migration. He wanted to limit the number of people who could settle in Britain from EU states. But Eurocrats told him that was no go. So instead he said he'd ban foreign nationals from claiming benefits for four years. People, the argument went, should put something into the pot before they drew payments from it. Again, Eurocrats said no.

By now, though, public expectations had been raised. David Cameron had to bring something back. An emergency brake on migration? No deal. A ban on benefits claims? No deal. OK, how about an emergency brake on benefits claims?

No, the EU would not give him even that. He had to make do with a promise of a phased and temporary introduction of welfare over four years. As for his manifesto promise to stop paying child benefit to kids who had never set foot in the United Kingdom, that, too, was abandoned, replaced by an agreement to pay it at a rate that more closely reflects the local cost of living – though even this will almost certainly be overturned in due course by the ECJ on grounds that it violates the right to freedom from discrimination by nationality guaranteed by EU citizenship.

I have recounted the story of the renegotiation in order to demonstrate quite how abject the surrender was. Having gone in with paltry and unassuming demands, the leader of the EU's second-largest contributor failed to get even those. He was forced to come back to his national parliament with what the Italians call 'fried air' – nothing at all.

If you think that is too harsh a summary, listen to how David Cameron concluded his statement to the House of Commons on 3 February 2016, announcing the package:

> We will:
>> never be part of the euro
>> never be part of Schengen
>> never be part of a European army
>> never be forced to bail out the eurozone with our taxpayers' money
>> and never be part of a European superstate
> That is the prize on offer.

Got that? The prime minister of the United Kingdom, the world's fifth-largest economy and fourth military power, was reduced to standing at the despatch box and boasting about the fact that he hadn't had to give anything else away. Even if all these things could be guaranteed – and, as we have seen, they can't – how do they possibly amount to a victory, an improvement on the previous position?

The whole process began, remember, because Britain was seeking better terms prior to its referendum. The prime minister went in looking for clear wins and came back with a restatement of the existing position – the position he had himself so recently been denouncing as unsatisfactory.

It all raises a very disquieting question. If this is how unwilling EU leaders are to make meaningful concessions now, when their second-largest member is about to vote on leaving, how much more intransigent will they become should that country vote to stay? If this is how they treat us now, when we might walk away and take our budget contributions with us, how would they treat us the day after we had voted to remain?

The renegotiation process was almost universally written off in Britain and in Brussels as nugatory, empty, a waste of time. But it wasn't a waste of time. It demonstrated, beyond all doubt, that the EU is unwilling or unable to change. Not only will it refuse to abandon its obsession with political union; it also won't allow any of its members to adopt a different status. The only way to get such a deal is from outside.

9

WHAT IS THE ALTERNATIVE?

'SO WHAT'S YOUR alternative?' demand Euro-enthusiasts. 'D'you want Britain to be like Norway? All cold and empty? Or like Switzerland? Making chocolate? And cuckoo clocks? That's what you want, is it? Eh, eh?'

The alternative to remaining in a structurally unsafe building is, of course, walking out; but I accept that this won't quite do as an answer. Although staying in the EU is a greater risk than leaving – the migration and euro crises are deepening, and Britain is being dragged into them – fear of change is deep in our genome, and we tend to vote accordingly.

Behavioural psychologists have written millions of words about risk-aversion. In test after test, given the chance to win something of greater value by staking something of lesser value, we make the mathematically irrational decision to stick with what we've got. As 'Remain' campaigners are well aware, referendums the world over tend to be won by whichever side is opposing change.

It's as true in the UK as anywhere else. Our two previous national referendums, on the EEC in 1975 and on changing the voting system in 2011, resulted in large majorities for the status quo. Scotland and Wales did vote for devolution in 1998 (having rejected it a generation earlier – albeit, in Scotland, by failing to reach the necessary threshold) but Scotland then voted against independence in 2014. Northern Ireland voted for the Belfast Agreement in 1998, having voted for the status quo in the 1973 border poll. London voted for a mayor in 1998, but North East England rejected devolution in 2004 – by such a decisive margin that the proposed referendums in other English regions were dropped. Since 2001, there have also been forty-seven referendums held by local authorities, of which thirty-three have gone against change. In total, then, 80 per cent of referendums in Britain have resulted in keeping the status quo.

Supporters of the EU can hardly be blamed, in the circumstances, for making change-aversion their key argument. They don't want to get drawn into arguments about democracy, or sovereignty, or the EU's declining share of the world economy, or border control, or Britain's budget contributions. They'd much rather conjure unspecific, inchoate fears about change.

On a purely tactical level, I can see the attraction. I've come across it again and again when debating with EU supporters. For example, I was recently in a discussion on Radio Ulster with a pro-EU politician from the Social Democratic and Labour Party (SDLP). The SDLP man was far too honest to try to argue that David Cameron had secured better terms from Brussels. Instead, he talked about what might go wrong following a 'Leave' vote. Would the border between the UK and the Republic of Ireland return? Would the peace process be jeopardized?

There is, of course, zero prospect of either thing happening, and I said so. London and Dublin have never enjoyed warmer relations than now. Even during the most rancorous moments in our history, there was never a closed border. Not only that, but much of the pre-partition structure remained in place. People weren't just free to move between the UK and Ireland; they took with them reciprocal voting rights and even mutual social security entitlements. Today, Ireland and the UK, which are in the EU, continue to form a border-free travel zone with the Isle of Man and the Channel Islands, which are outside the EU. So why on Earth, after ninety-five years without a border, inside and outside the EU, should there be one now?

How did he respond to these points, the amiable SDLP man? As pro-EU campaigners so often do in such a situation. 'Yeah, Daniel, you could well be right. But why take the risk?' It may be an intellectually weak argument but, by Heaven, it's emotionally powerful.

Understandably, fear of the unknown has become the mainstay of the 'Remain' case. As one pro-EU friend, a Conservative MP, put it to me: 'It's like the banks. Everyone moans about their bank. But how many people take their accounts elsewhere?'

Well, you'd move your account pretty sharpish if you thought the bank might fail. The truth is that there is no status quo in this referendum. A vote to leave will result in a trade-only deal with the EU – membership of a common market, not a common government. A vote to stay will be a vote to be part of the continuing political, fiscal and military integration of the EU. As we see that the euro and migration crises are deteriorating, that future can hardly be called risk-averse. Voting to leave is the safer option.

So, to return to the question which opened the chapter, what is the alternative? Well, all the options involve remaining part of the European free trade zone that stretches from non-EU Iceland to non-EU Turkey. Since the Moldova and Ukraine Association Agreements came into effect in 2014, only two European states stand outside this tariff-free nexus: Russia and Belarus.

No one in Brussels argues that Britain would have to leave that common market if it left the EU. Nor, in fairness, do Remainers, if you listen carefully. Instead, they talk about jobs being 'dependent on our trade with the EU', hoping that at least some voters will hear that line as 'dependent on our membership of the EU'.

When every non-EU territory from the Faroe Islands to Montenegro has access to the European free trade area, it would be preposterous beyond words to claim that the UK, uniquely, would be denied full market access. This is especially true when we consider the balance of UK–EU trade.

As Figure Eight shows, Britain's trade with the EU is in deficit and shrinking, while her trade with the rest of the world is in surplus and growing. Over the entire period of her membership, the United Kingdom has run an overall surplus with the rest of the world but a

Fig. 8

IN SURPLUS WITH EVERYONE
EXCEPT THE EU

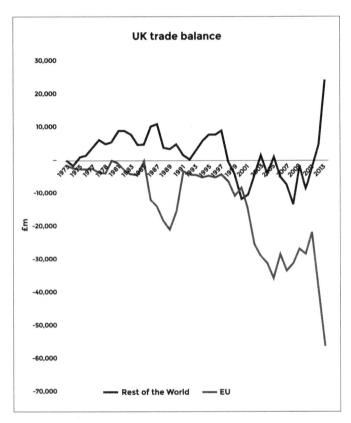

Source: ONS data

big deficit with Europe. In other words, she has had to make up in her sales to the Americas, Africa, Asia and Australia what she has lost in her trade with Europe.

A deficit is not, intrinsically, a bad thing. The fact that Britain buys more from the rest of the EU than she sells there is in no sense an argument against such trade from Britain's point of view. Tariffs and trade barriers are always and everywhere detrimental to the overall performance of a country's economy, for all that they may temporarily benefit one sector within that country.

The point of these figures is simply to demonstrate how absurd is the claim that Britain's participation in European markets would be jeopardized by her non-participation in the various political structures in Brussels. Although we often ask how much EU trade matters to Britain, we less often ask how much British trade matters to the EU.

According to HMRC, Britain bought from the other twenty-seven EU members more than she sold to them to the value of £59 billion in 2014. On leaving, the UK would instantly become the EU's single largest export destination, worth £289 billion. It is very rare, in any negotiation, for the salesman to bully or threaten the customer.

To illustrate the absurdity of citing the three million British jobs linked to EU trade as being in some way sustained by membership, let's imagine that statistic the other way around. How many jobs in the EU are linked to trade with the UK? I've noticed already during this referendum campaign that many EU supporters talk as if EU states chose to trade with Britain out of kindness. They might care to glance at Figure Nine.

Three million British jobs are not in any way linked to membership of the EU. The academic on whose research that claim was based, Dr Martin Weale, has described it as 'pure Goebbels'. If we were to apply the same reasoning, then five million EU jobs are dependent on Britain. But, in reality, none of these jobs is actually at stake – except possibly mine and those of a few hundred British Eurocrats.

Even if the other EU states wanted to act from sheer spite (which seems unlikely), and even if the WTO rules made it easy to impose a tariff where there previously wasn't one (which they don't) and even if there were examples of other geographically European states facing tariffs when they trade with the EU (which there aren't), it would still make absolutely no sense for the Continental EU states to restrict the cross-Channel trade of which they are the chief beneficiaries.

So, if all the options involve remaining in the free market – which even leading 'Remain' campaigners, including the prime minister and Lord Rose accept – which particular model should we follow? Isle of Man? Monaco? Macedonia? Who?

It's important to note that all non-EU countries within the European area have their own particular deals with the EU. No two are identical. So it would be silly to say that Britain should precisely copy Iceland or Switzerland or any other foreign example. Like every other state, Britain will negotiate her own deal on departure, tailored to suit her own conditions and needs.

It is nonetheless worth considering what some of the non-EU states do, if only to give ourselves a rough idea of what a trade-based deal – half-in and half-out, to quote the obligatory cliché – actually looks like.

I began this book by saying that Norway, Iceland and Switzerland were arguably the most useful comparators in the sense that they were neither micro-states nor countries recovering from the calamity of communism. Before we look in more detail at what they do, though, we should stress that no one is suggesting that Britain slavishly mimic any of them. Each country has unique circumstances. Britain is, most obviously, far larger than any of these states, in terms of population, economic strength and global reach. She runs a structural trade deficit with the EU,

Fig. 9

WHO NEEDS WHOM?

421,000 jobs

494,000 jobs

309,000 jobs

France exported €1.3bn worth of wine to the UK in 2013

Spain exported €740m worth of fruit to the UK in 2013

Source: House of Commons Library, 2011 Figures, IMF and UN Comtrade

Germany exported €16bn worth of cars to the UK in 2013

million jobs

The UK is the EU's single largest market – in 2013 the EU exported **€280 billion** worth of goods to the UK. Neither side will have any appetite for a 'trade war'

Italy exported €500m worth of shoes to the UK in 2013

whereas they tend to run surpluses. She exports a lower percentage of her goods and services to the EU than they do. And, of course, these three countries all differ one from another. Switzerland, for example, has a much higher population during office hours than it has at weekends: many EU citizens commute from Austria, Germany, France and Italy to work in the Helvetic Confederation. There were therefore arguments of convenience and ease of movement there that supported Swiss membership of Schengen. Plainly, such arguments don't apply to seagirt Britain, and no one is seriously suggesting that the United Kingdom join that system.

To remind you, all three of these countries – members of the European Free Trade Association (EFTA) – prefer their current deal to ours: 60 per cent of Icelanders, 79 per cent of Norwegians and 82 per cent of Swiss oppose EU membership.

Who can blame them? Norway and Switzerland are, according to the Legatum Institute's prosperity index, the wealthiest and second-wealthiest nations on Earth. Money isn't everything, of course. Still, it's worth noting that the UN's Human Development Index, which takes account of literacy, longevity and the like, has a similar line-up: Norway first, Australia second, Switzerland third.

All the EFTA countries score highly by global standards. Despite being badly hit in the 2008 financial crash, Iceland has returned to 16th place in the UN's quality of life index, and 12th in Legatum's – and it is rising fast in both. There is an important difference, though, between, on the one hand, Iceland and Norway – which are members of the European Economic Area (EEA) – and on the other, Switzerland – which is in EFTA only.

The EEA was established in 1992 as a waiting room for the EU. At that time, its members were expected to join the EU in the referendums scheduled in 1994. Three EFTA states – Austria, Finland and Sweden – did indeed vote to join. But stubborn, sturdy Norway again voted for independence. No one at that time imagined that, twenty-four years later, Norway, having rejected EU membership, would still be in the EEA.

Because the EEA was supposed to be a transitional arrangement, it contained a mechanism for the automatic adoption of EU legislation. This made sense as an accelerated way to harmonize the legal systems of the EFTA states swiftly in the run-up to membership. It was never designed to be permanent.

It is this aspect of the EEA that EU supporters keep gasping and swooning over, with all the theatricality

Fig. 10

LEGATUM PROSPERITY INDEX 2015

1		Norway
2		Switzerland
3		Denmark
4		New Zealand
5		Sweden
6 =		Canada
6 =		Australia
8		Netherlands
9 =		Finland
9 =		Ireland

Fig. 11

UNITED NATIONS HUMAN DEVELOPMENT INDEX 2015

1		Norway
2		Australia
3		Switzerland
4		Denmark
5		Netherlands
6 =		Germany
6 =		Ireland
8		United States
9 =		Canada
9 =		New Zealand

of Victorian matrons. It is, we keep being told, a form of 'fax diplomacy'. Those poor, chilly Norwegians are to be pictured waiting by their fax machines for the latest instructions to come bleeping through from Brussels.

Never mind the archaic metaphor: we know that Little Europeans are nostalgists at heart. The charge is that Norway has only a consultative role, and no formal vote, in some EU regulations that it must later enforce.

But this is more a problem in theory than in practice. According to the EFTA Secretariat, the EU generated 52,183 legal instruments between 2000 and 2013, of which Norway adopted 4,724 – 9 per cent. And many of these rules were minor technical standards: fewer than 100 of those 4,724 legal instruments required primary legislation in the Norwegian parliament, or *Storting*.

A written answer to a parliamentary question in Iceland found a similar proportion: 6,326 out of 62,809 EU legal acts between 1994 and 2014. Yet, rather than use the official statistics, Europhiles have seized on a stray remark by a Euro-fanatical Norwegian minister to the effect that 'three-quarters of our laws' come from Brussels, and have solemnly translated that throwaway line into an official-sounding '75 per cent'.

In Switzerland, there is no ambiguity: the figure

is zero per cent. The Swiss sometimes copy EU regulations for reasons of economy of scale, though more often both Switzerland and the EU are adopting global rules. But, though Swiss exporters must meet EU standards when selling to the EU (just as they must meet Japanese standards when selling to Japan), they generally don't apply those standards to their domestic economy. Britain, by contrast, must apply 100 per cent of EU regulations to 100 per cent of its economy.

Switzerland is not a full participant in the single market in services. This doesn't mean, obviously, that UBS can't operate in Frankfurt, but it does mean that Swiss financial institutions are not part of the same regulatory structure as those in the EU. If they want to trade there, they must adopt different rules. The flip-side, of course, is that Zurich doesn't need to worry about the expensive and sometimes downright malicious EU regulations that menace London: the Alternative Investment Fund Managers Directive, the short-selling ban, the Financial Transactions Tax.

Why does Switzerland have a better deal than Norway? Because Swiss politicians, habituated to their country's tradition of direct democracy, accepted the verdict of their referendum in a way that their Norwegian counterparts never truly did. Although most Swiss parties and politicians had wanted EU membership, and campaigned for membership of the EEA as a step towards accession, they accepted defeat with good grace. That's what happens in a country whose rules render politicians representatives and not rulers.

In Norway, by contrast, the pro-EU parties never stopped hankering after eventual membership. Norwegian politicians – including the present prime minister and, indeed, that rabidly pro-Brussels Europe minister whom the BBC like to trot out – know that replacing the EEA with a more permanent deal would mean formally accepting that membership was off the agenda, and that their country could no longer think of itself as a long-term candidate. A cynic might say that the one-sidedness of the EEA – the 'fax diplomacy' – suits them, because it strengthens the case for full membership vis-à-vis their own voters.

Happily, though, the Norwegian people are wiser than their leaders. They know that, imperfect as it necessarily is, the EEA is still preferable to full membership. As a result of public opinion, EU accession is completely off the agenda, in Norway as in Switzerland.

The gap between people and politicians might also explain why Norway pays more, per capita, into the EU budget than its fellow EFTA states. Norwegian ministers like to opt in to as many common EU projects as possible, on everything from research and development to foreign aid. They are under no treaty obligation to participate in these projects: Iceland joined the EEA on the same terms but declines to join in.

Some years ago, I travelled to both Oslo and Reykjavík and asked officials in the two governments why there was such a wide discrepancy in participation fees. The Norwegian bureaucrats gave me a long answer about how wonderful the EU's Horizon project on university research was, and how sensible it was to have a unified approach to international development. The Icelanders were pithier: 'Because those Norwegians are f***ing crazy.'

According to Professor Herman Matthijs of Brussels Free University, who has produced the only like-with-like comparator, Iceland's annual per capita contribution is 50 euros, Switzerland's 68 and Norway's 107. These figures include a contribution to the running of the Schengen Area, which no one is suggesting that Britain join. The United Kingdom's current per capita annual payment, by the same methodology, is 229 euros.

How much would Britain pay after leaving? Plainly, there would be a small administrative cost to cover the functioning of the institutions that invigilate the free market. The EFTA states contribute to a Surveillance Authority and a Tribunal that polices tariff-free commerce across the EFTA and EU zone. They also agreed to pay a fee, phased in, to the new EU states to help them meet the cost of adopting EU standards. Beyond that, they opt in to some joint projects and not others, and Britain would presumably be free to do the same.

For example, representatives of British universities often talk about the financial support they get from the EU. In fact, this is from schemes that are not exclusive to EU states. The Horizon Programme, the main vehicle for joint university research funding, covers as full participants not only the EU states and Norway, but also Canada and Israel, and operates in more than 100 additional states and territories. Whether a post-Brexit UK would wish to remain a full participant would, of course, be up to British universities and ministers. There is an argument that, as with the Common Fisheries Policy, Britain is filling the pot disproportionately and would be better off funding her own tertiary education sector directly rather than routing the money through Brussels – see Figure Twelve.

On the other hand, there may be advantages of scale in continuing participation. (Plainly, the people who

Fig. 12

ADVANTAGE ANGLOSPHERE

Times Higher Education World University Rankings 2015/16

1	California Institute of Technology, US
2	University of Oxford, UK
3	Stanford University, US
4	University of Cambridge, UK
5	Massachusetts Institute of Technology, US
6	Harvard University, US
7	Princeton University, US
8	Imperial College London, UK
9	ETH Zürich – Swiss Federal Institute of Technology Zurich, Switzerland
10	University of Chicago, US
11	Johns Hopkins University, US
12	Yale University, US
13	University of California, Berkeley, US
14	University College London, UK
15	Columbia University, US
16	University of California, Los Angeles, US
17	University of Pennsylvania, US
18	Cornell University, US
19	University of Toronto, Canada
20	Duke University, US

allocate the existing funding, and whose livelihoods depend on the current system, will not find it easy to be objective about this choice.) But British universities as a whole may prefer to remain involved, in which case, clearly, our financial contributions would rise accordingly.

It's striking, incidentally, that of the world's top universities, fourteen are in the United States, four in the United Kingdom and none in the rest of the EU. This should put into context the idea that British higher education somehow needs European support.

What goes for universities goes for other areas, too. A post-EU Britain could decide, as other non-EU states do, where it wanted to remain involved. Unlike other non-EU countries, it would be starting from a position of involvement which, for personal and organizational reasons, might create more of a bias, on both sides, to continuing participation. But it would be up to a future government to make the final decision.

For example, there might be a case for remaining involved with Europol, the EU's policing agency. Fourteen non-EU states co-operate with that body, based in The Hague: Albania, Australia, Canada, Colombia, Iceland, Liechtenstein, Macedonia, Moldova, Monaco, Montenegro, Norway, Serbia, Switzerland and the United States.

On the other hand, Europol was explicitly created to become (as the European Parliament put it at the time) the EU's 'federal police force'. While it has not yet secured that status, it has been gradually extending its powers seeking, as the FBI did in its early days, to establish its jurisdiction over certain categories of crime: people trafficking, money laundering, certain Internet crimes. Britain may decide that she is happier simply working through Interpol.

The point is that, either way, it would be for a future British government to decide. When people ask 'Leave' campaigners to set out their alternative in detail, they are inviting us to behave as if we were in office. But we're not. It'll be for the United Kingdom's elected representatives to set the precise terms and conditions of our future relations with the EU. All we can do is set out some broad, obvious guidelines: we'd retain free trade with the single market; we'd withdraw from the Common Agricultural and Fisheries Policies; our laws would be supreme on our own territory; we'd apply no tariffs, either to EU or non-EU states; we'd remain outside Schengen; we'd stay in NATO and the Council of Europe.

To move beyond these principles into detailed policy questions – How much funding would universities get? Would we keep the EU rules on paid holidays? –

is to usurp the role of an elected British Parliament. The whole purpose of withdrawal is to let the British people decide such questions for themselves again.

When we look at the EFTA countries, we see, not an exact model to follow, but a happy vision of how well a country can do engaging in free trade with the EU rather than political amalgamation.

Now here's the clinching statistic. The EU takes 55 per cent of Swiss exports, and 81 per cent of Norwegian exports, as opposed to 45 per cent of British exports. As we have seen, Europhiles like to claim that 'around' half our exports go to the EU, but that figure has fallen by 10 per cent since 2006. How much lower must it go before we drop the idea that we need to merge our political institutions?

To summarize, then, Norway gets a better deal than Britain currently does, and Switzerland a better deal than Norway. But a post-EU Britain, with 65 million people to Switzerland's eight and Norway's five, should expect something better yet. We are far less dependent on the EU than these states: Norway's exports to the EU, per head of population, are two-and-a-half times ours; Switzerland's four-and-a-half times.

Now, a caveat. The very fact of mentioning Norway and Switzerland will lead to two contradictory responses from the pro-EU campaign. First, they will fix on something about those countries that no one proposes to copy and try to make the argument about that thing. 'Ah, so you want to join Schengen, do you?' Second, and contradictorily, they will say that those two states have nothing to teach us. 'How can you possibly compare us to Switzerland?'

In politics, whenever you offer a foreign example, in however narrow and limited a context, you are guaranteed – guaranteed – to be told an unrelated fact about the country you've cited. You admire Estonia's approach to shale extraction? 'You can't compare us to Estonia: they've got Putin on their border.' You think Singapore has got a useful system of individual health-care accounts? 'Yeah, and I suppose you want to live in a semi-dictatorship.' We might usefully learn from Sweden's school voucher system? 'Britain isn't Sweden!'

Likewise, the idea that Norway and Switzerland illustrate how a country can thrive inside Europe's common market but outside the EU, never fails to raise the classic response.

'You can't compare us to Norway, they've got oil and fish!' Well, OK. I mean, Britain has oil and, but for the wretched EU, we'd have fish, too. Still, if you really don't like Norway, what about Switzerland? It has no natural resources to speak of. Like us, the Swiss became world leaders in financial services: maybe that's a useful parallel? 'Yeah, well, the Swiss took Nazi gold!'

I won't argue the point. I'll just offer my last-ditch example. If Norway and Switzerland are too exotic for you, how about Guernsey? If we can't draw a parallel even with the Channel Islands, we are truly lost to introversion and solipsism. Guernsey is an English-speaking, common law, parliamentary democracy. Its currency is the pound. Its head of state is the Queen. It is, for certain purposes, in political union with the UK. Its political system resembles ours in every way. Except one. Guernsey is outside the EU.

The Bailiwick isn't a precise model for us, obviously, any more than any of the EFTA countries is. But it surely offers some lessons about how countries in a trade-only relationship with the EU can flourish.

Essentially, Guernsey opts in to the economic aspects of EU membership but opts out of everything else. Under Protocol 3 of the UK's accession treaty, the Channel Islands are covered by the EU's trade and tariffs policies. But they are outside the Common Fisheries Policy, outside the Common Agricultural Policy (except for import duties on non-EU produce) and outside the common rules on justice, home affairs, foreign policy, employment law and environmental regulation.

Guernsey is part of a free-movement area with the UK and Ireland, but controls immigration from the rest of the EU. Indeed, startlingly to British eyes, it has an immigration policy: its legislators vote on whom to admit, on what terms and in what numbers. They are currently, for example, debating how many Syrian refugees they might take in. They set an annual population target, and issue their residence permits accordingly, mainly taking in temporary workers from Latvia and Madeira.

Parliamentary sovereignty evidently suits the Guerns. Their economy has been growing steadily at around 3 per cent a year, their GDP per capita is one of the highest in the world, unemployment is in the hundreds and crime is virtually non-existent.

I can already hear the scoffers. 'You can't compare us to Guernsey: it's tiny.' Look, let's nail down this surprisingly common objection. Are we seriously supposed to think that small nations can thrive outside the EU but large ones can't? It's extraordinary how quickly EU supporters switch from 'Britain has to be part of a bigger bloc' to 'You can't compare us to small countries'. Apparently we're simultaneously too large and too small to prosper.

'Ah, but Guernsey is a tax haven.' In the sense that it has low taxes, yes. And why does it have low taxes?

Because it is well-governed. As late as the 1980s, Guernsey had no financial services industry, and its economy rested on tomatoes and tourism. Since then, it has built up a highly successful services sector without being covered by most EU directives. That's the really key point. Like Switzerland, but unlike the UK, Guernsey is excluded from some aspects of the single market in services. But the flip-side is that it doesn't have to apply idiotic Brussels rules that threaten managed funds and smaller banks.

Guernsey's relationship with the EU is not perfect. Many of its business leaders and politicians complain that the UK government is pressuring them to accept too many EU-inspired rules in areas from fish quotas to financial regulation. Still, at least they have the right to say no – unlike Britain, where EU law has primacy and where these rules are enacted automatically.

To repeat, we shouldn't aim to replicate Guernsey's deal. For example, our global trade links give us more incentive to be able to negotiate bilateral deals outside the Common Commercial Policy. Still, an economics-only deal, inside the market but outside the political structures, is attractive.

The chief minister of Guernsey is a hugely impressive man called Jonathan Le Tocq, one of the last islanders to have been brought up speaking the local Norman French dialect. He studied in Paris and feels very European. But what he prizes above all is the sense of accountability intrinsic in the island's parliamentary system. 'People know that they're in control,' he told me. 'If they don't like a policy, they can get it changed.' Extraordinary, really, that such a thing should need saying. Extraordinary that Britain – which developed and exported the sublime idea that laws should not be passed, nor taxes raised, except by elected representatives – should now look enviously at its Crown possessions off the Norman coast.

To summarize then, the alternative to EU membership is an association deal based on free trade and intergovernmental co-operation. We'll recover our parliamentary sovereignty and, with it, the ability to sign bilateral trade agreements with non-EU countries, as Norway and Switzerland do – an increasingly important advantage when every continent in the world is growing except Antarctica and Europe. We'd obviously remain outside Schengen.

Why should the other member states allow Britain such a deal? Because it would be in everyone's interest. The UK runs a structural deficit with the EU, only partly offset by its surplus with the rest of the world. On the day we left, we would immediately become the EU's biggest export market. The idea that either side would wish to jeopardize the flow of cross-Channel trade is bizarre. And, in any case, it is remarkably difficult, under WTO rules, to apply a trade barrier where you previously didn't have one.

Many European federalists actively campaign for Britain to be given an economics-only relationship – what Jacques Delors calls 'privileged partnership' and Guy Verhofstadt 'associate membership'. It would allow them to push ahead with a European army, a common tax system and so on, while Britain led an outer tier of some twenty European states and territories, part of a common market but not a common government.

We now know that such a deal can't be struck from inside. Or, at the very least, that the other members won't entertain it as long as they think the United Kingdom isn't serious about withdrawal.

All that is needed is self-confidence. Are we prepared to use our faculty for reason rather than be swayed by the risk-aversion that evolved in our genome in Pleistocene Africa? Are we prepared to aim, calmly and reasonably, for an economics-based deal that would suit both sides better than the current rancour?

'Iceland is much better off outside the EU,' says prime minister Sigmundur Davíð Gunnlaugsson. 'Unemployment is minimal, purchasing power has never been higher, and we have control over our own legal framework, currency and natural resources.'

Quite. Iceland has a population of 320,000. The United Kingdom has 65 million people. Can't we manage to run our own affairs?

10

BETTER OFF OUT

I F YOU TOT up all your household bills, which are the main ones? Obviously, it depends on circumstances: for some it's the mortgage payments or the rent, for others the cost of running the car. For most of us, though, three items are at or near the top of the list: food bills, fuel bills and taxes.

Taxes are the item we tend to overlook, because they are dispersed and disguised. We don't always notice what we're paying through VAT or PAYE – although, if we consolidated all our tax bills, they would probably be the single largest item.

So let's start close to home. What would be the impact of leaving the EU on these three chief components of the average family budget? All, surely, would be lower after withdrawal.

Taxation is the easiest to quantify. According to the Office for Budgetary Responsibility (OBR), Britain's contribution to the EU in 2016 will be £19.6 billion gross or £11.1 billion net.[37] Since we are measuring the impact on taxation, it is the gross figure that is relevant here. Sure, some of the money Britain hands over to the EU is returned or spent in this country. But, when measuring tax, we don't deduct notional value. Ask your neighbours how much their council tax bill is. I doubt they'll subtract the value of the bin collection and the street lighting.

So what does £19.6 billion amount to? According to the Institute for Fiscal Studies (IFS), it is equivalent to the combined revenue of Vehicle Excise (£5.9 billion), Capital Gains Tax (£5.4 billion), Air Passenger Duty (£3.2 billion), Inheritance Tax (£3.9 billion) and Petroleum Tax (£1.2 billion). To put it another way, it would allow the entire country to get a 71 per cent rebate in council tax (which raises £27.6 billion).

If you prefer to look at spending, then perhaps the best way to contextualize the cost of the EU is as follows. According to the IFS, the combined savings made by all the departmental spending cuts during

37 OBR Economic and Fiscal Outlook, November 2015

the 2010 to 2015 parliament was £35 billion. Treasury figures indicate that our gross contribution to the EU over the same period was £86 billion – more than twice as much as was saved by the austerity programme across the whole of domestic spending. Even if we insist on deducting the money that was spent in the UK, our net contribution was still £45.4 billion over the lifetime of that parliament. How odd that, during all the marches against austerity, all the UK Uncut protests, all the furious editorials about 'Tory cuts', no one pointed out that one clean excision, using the gross figure, would have reversed the entire cuts programme and still allowed us to take a penny off income tax.

So much for our tax bills. What about our household bills? These are necessarily harder to quantify, and people will understandably be jaded by the figures flying back and forth between the 'Leave' and 'Remain' camps. For example, the organization Business for Britain published a massive half-million-word study which concluded that the average household might be better off by £933 a year as a result of lower prices outside the EU.[38] But, with pro-EU groups claiming the opposite, readers will naturally be cynical.

What seems undeniable is that, for food and fuel

38 'Change, or Go', 2015

bills – the two largest household bills for most of us, after tax – any change would be downward.

Britain is unusual in the EU, being a food importer with relatively large and efficient farms. She has always been penalized both positively and negatively by the Common Agricultural Policy (CAP), paying more into the system than other states and getting less out of it. It was mainly because of this structural imbalance that, in 1984, Margaret Thatcher secured a partial rebate in Britain's budget contributions – partial because it works as a percentage of the difference between contributions and receipts, and therefore only operates to the extent that Britain is being adversely affected.

As we have seen, before 1973, the United Kingdom was in the habit of importing food and commodities from outside Europe. Some historians talk of the 'ghost acres' in her colonies that allowed her to specialize in services and industry while importing wheat from Canada and meat and butter from Australia and New Zealand. After 1973, as the CAP was applied to Britain, she moved away from purchasing food at world prices and increased her dependence on imports from other EEC states. Food prices rose sharply, especially meat and dairy products and cereals.

Labour Eurosceptics, in particular, had campaigned against 'dearer food', arguing that an increase in grocery bills was, in reality, a form of regressive tax that hit the poor hardest, since food represented a higher proportion of their household expenditure. They objected, too, to the impact on exporters in developing countries, especially in Africa, who found that their chief markets were closed to them by EEC protectionism. Indeed, in many cases, poorer countries were not only impoverished by EEC protectionism, but were also hit by dumping. Output-based subsidies produced European wine lakes and butter mountains, which were sometimes sold at below-cost price to poorer countries, wiping out the one sector on which their export earnings would otherwise have depended.

Although some of the abuses in the CAP have been tackled, food prices in Europe remain well above world levels. Britain is still one of the countries that suffers most from the CAP, which accounts for 40 per cent of the EU budget, and consumes £4.6 billion of the UK's gross contribution to the EU. The CAP then pays British farmers some £2.9 billion.[39] It would, in other words, be possible not only to maintain the current level of support to British farmers, but handsomely to increase it while still making a substantial saving for the nation.

How precisely this would happen would, of course,

39 House of Lords, answer to written question HL3254,
   3 November 2015

be for a future government to determine, but the broad principle of protecting our countryside – and compensating its guardians for maintaining our natural heritage – is fairly uncontentious. My own preference would be to offer all British farmers a straightforward grant of £90 per acre, regardless of land quality or total acreage. This payment would, in effect, recognize that they are not able to realize the full value of their land by selling it as housing or turning it into a golf course. Because it was a straight grant, it would be cheap and easy to administer – and, as important, easy to claim. British farmers, if my experiences as a constituency MEP are anything to go by, are resigned, not only to complex form-filling, but to frequent bureaucratic snarl-ups and delays. As I write, many of my farming constituents have had to run up overdrafts because of long delays in the processing of the 2015 grants.

While £90 an acre would leave almost all our farmers better off and able to compete on a level playing field in world markets, the end of the CAP would see British food prices fall back towards non-EU levels as tariffs and quotas were dropped. The fall in household bills would act as a stimulus to the entire economy, and the return to the global trading system would facilitate trade agreements with non-EU producers, thus opening opportunities for, among others, British farmers.

As for food, so for energy: the gains to consumers would also be gains for the UK as a whole. We would benefit both directly (we'd have more left in our bank accounts each month) and indirectly (the economy would be growing faster).

As a result of EU policy, we have some of the highest electricity and gas bills in the world. Brussels drives up prices in two ways: through setting renewables targets and, since 2010, through direct legislation. As a result, a medium-sized business in the EU pays 20 per cent more for energy than an equivalent firm in China, 65 per cent more than one in India and 100 per cent more than one in the United States.[40] These artificially high energy prices have already closed down almost the whole of Britain's steel industry and now threaten other high-energy manufacturing sectors. And not just our businesses: in 2012–2013, the NHS spent an extraordinary £630 million on energy bills.[41]

It is of course true that the world is seeking to reduce carbon emissions, and Britain would presumably remain part of that global effort inside or outside the EU. But the EU doesn't simply set a target for emissions cuts and leave it to the member states to meet it.

40 European Commission Staff Working Document, 'Energy prices and costs report', 17 March 2014
41 TaxPayers' Alliance, *Research Note 133: Energy and Water Bills in the NHS*, 21 November 2013

That would be to accept the supremacy of the approach agreed at the 2015 Paris Climate Summit which, being global, makes regional blocs largely irrelevant. Instead, Brussels supports specific forms of alternative energy in a way that has the incidental effect of purchasing the loyalty of those who supply it.

Where I live, in beautiful countryside on the Hampshire–Berkshire borders, upper-class welfarism is surprisingly widespread. The talk at dinner parties will often turn to (say) how you can get £30,000 a year from the government by installing a woodchip boiler, which can then conveniently be used to heat your swimming pool. Because most alternative energy schemes benefit people who own land, woods and suitable sites for wind farms, they end up becoming a form of regressive taxation. People on low and medium incomes pay higher electricity bills to subsidize land-owners – who, in many cases, then become a powerful and articulate pro-EU lobby. Not in every case, of course: there are Eurosceptic landowners, just as there are MEPs who want to put themselves out of work. But you can see why, from a pro-EU point of view, the current system is attractive.

What it is far less useful for is reducing carbon emissions. As Friends of the Earth points out, the impact of EU policy is, in effect, to force manufacturers and other businesses to outsource to places with far lower environmental standards. British industrialists naturally agree. So, come to that, does the British Government. According to a study by the department for energy and climate change, just two EU rules are responsible for 9 per cent of the energy costs incurred by energy-intensive businesses today – a figure that will rise to 16 per cent in 2030.[42]

The closure of Britain's steel mills in 2015 may be a grisly foretaste of what is to come. Although campaigners from the industry focused on Britain's inability to activate anti-dumping rules against China – because, as we have seen, Britain has no vote on the WTO, being instead represented there by the European Commission – the far more serious problem was the uncompetitive energy prices that place British manufacturers at a disadvantage vis-à-vis non-EU competitors.

Which industry will be next? Paper mills? Glass? Ceramics? Cement? Or perhaps the chemical industry, already hobbled by the EU's REACH directive which, exactly like the energy directives, in effect forces importers to purchase stock from non-EU sources with less onerous regulations?

42 'Estimated impacts of energy and climate change policies on energy prices and bills', Department of Energy & Climate Change, 2013

The point is that, as long as British businesses are regulated from abroad, we cannot ensure that they operate within a framework tailored to suit their own needs.

Cutting taxes, food bills and fuel bills will give the economy a far more effective and durable stimulus than quantitative easing ever did. And, unlike that policy, which disproportionately favoured wealthier people with assets, this would be a highly progressive policy, of most benefit to low-income households, a greater proportion of whose resources go on staples. Since poorer households are likelier to alter their behaviour when their disposable income increases, the stimulus effect is greater.

It's worth dwelling on the advantage of lower bills because it illustrates something that is in danger of being overlooked in this referendum campaign, namely the optimistic case for withdrawal. The way in which broadcasters, in particular, like to frame the debate is as sovereignty versus convenience, or people versus business.

In fact, the strongest case for voting to leave is that it offers a better future. Not just a safer future. Not just a more democratic future. Not just a future where Britain's pride, confidence and global links are restored. We'd be better off in the literal, financial sense.

Pause for a moment and let the vision of an independent Britain take form in your mind's eye.

It's 2020, and the UK is flourishing outside of the EU. The rump Union, now a united bloc, continues its genteel decline, but Britain has become the most successful and competitive knowledge-based economy in the region. Our universities attract the world's brightest students. We lead the way in software, biotech, law, finance and the audio-visual sector. We have forged a distinctive foreign policy, allied to Europe, but giving due weight to the US, India and other common-law, Anglophone democracies.

More intangibly but no less significantly, we have recovered our self-belief. As Nicolas Sarkozy, president of the European Federation, crossly puts it: 'In economic terms, Britain is Hong Kong to Europe's China, Singapore to our Indonesia.'

Part of our success rests on bilateral free-trade agreements with the rest of the world. The EU has to weigh the interests of Italian textile manufacturers, French film-makers, Polish farmers. Even Germany likes to defend its analogue-era giants against American Internet challengers such as Google, Amazon, Facebook and Uber.

Once outside the Common External Tariff, the UK swiftly signed a slew of free-trade agreements, including with the US, India and Australia. Our policy is like Switzerland's: we match EU trade negotiators when convenient, but go further when Brussels is reluctant to liberalize, as with China. Following Switzerland, we forged overseas relationships while remaining full members of the EU's common market – covered by free movement of goods, services and capital.

Non-EU trade matters more than ever. Since 2010, every region in the world has experienced significant economic growth – except Europe. The prosperity of distant continents has spilled over into Britain. Our Atlantic ports, above all Glasgow and Liverpool, are entering a second golden age.

London, too, is booming. Eurocrats never had much sympathy for financial services. As their regulations took effect – a financial transactions tax, a ban on short-selling, restrictions on clearing, a bonus cap, windfall levies, micro-regulation of funds – waves of young financiers brought their talents from Frankfurt, Paris and Milan to the City.

Other EU regulations, often little known, had caused enormous damage. The REACH Directive, limiting chemical products, imposed huge costs on manufacturers. The bans on vitamin supplements and herbal remedies had closed down many health shops. London's art market had been brutalized by EU rules on VAT and retrospective taxation. All these sectors have revived. So have older industries. Our farmers, freed from the CAP, are world-beating. Our fisheries are once again a great renewable resource. Disapplying the EU's rules on data management made Hoxton the global capital for software design. Scrapping EU rules on clinical trials allowed Britain to recover its place as a world leader in medical research.

Universities no longer waste their time on Kafka-esque EU grant applications. Now, they compete on quality, attracting talent from every continent and charging accordingly.

Immigration is keenly debated. Every year, Parliament votes on how many permits to make available for students, medical workers and refugees. Every would-be migrant can compete on an equal basis: the rules that privileged Europeans over Commonwealth citizens, often with family links to Britain, were dropped immediately after independence.

Britain has been able to tap into her huge reserves of shale gas and oil, which came on tap, almost providentially, just as North Sea gas was running out, and with all the infrastructure thus in place. At the same time, the free-trade deal with China has led to the import of cheap solar panels, which the EU had banned. They are now so integrated into buildings and vehicles that we barely notice them. Cheaper energy means lower production costs, more competitive exports and a boom all round.

Unsurprisingly, several other European states have opted for a similar deal. Some (Norway, Switzerland) came from the old European Free Trade Association; others (Sweden, Denmark) from the EU; yet others (Turkey, Georgia) from further afield. The United Kingdom leads a twenty-one-state bloc that forms a common market with the EU 25, but remains outside their political structures. The EU 25, meanwhile, have pushed ahead with full integration, including a European army and police force and harmonized taxes, prompting Ireland and the Netherlands to announce referendums on whether to follow Britain.

Best of all, we have cast off the pessimism that infected us during our EU years, the sense that we were too small to make a difference. As we left, we shook our heads, looked about, and realized that we were the fifth-largest economy on Earth, the fourth military power, a leading member of the G7, a permanent seat-holder on the UN Security Council, and home to the world's greatest city and most widely spoken language. We knew that we had plenty more to give.

CONCLUSION

TWO ROADS DIVERGED

VOTING TO STAY in the EU is not the same as voting to stay where we are. The EU, as we have seen, is a process, a dynamic. Its leaders, unlike most British Euro-integrationists, are admirably frank about where they are heading. They want to complete an undertaking that their predecessors began in 1956, and whose aims they keep reiterating (see Appendix One). They want the nations of Europe to federate, ceding control over the larger questions of foreign affairs, economics, security, human rights and citizenship to Brussels institutions.

This doesn't mean that the nations will be completely abolished, any more than the federation of the thirteen American states in 1787 meant the abolition of Pennsylvania. Pennsylvania retained, and retains, her legislature, her state government and her flag. Indeed, in some senses, Pennsylvania has more freedom of action within the US than Britain has within the EU: she can set her own indirect taxes, for example, and can decide whether or not to apply the death penalty. But no one would seriously call Pennsylvania an independent country.

The EU is moving towards eventual federation. As we have seen, it doesn't need any further legal changes to reach that destination. It has already given itself all the requisite powers including, since the Lisbon Treaty came into effect in 2009, a self-amending mechanism, which allows it to extend its jurisdiction without getting the permission of all the member governments.

Imagine that you are on a bus – a bus whose destination, a United States of Europe, is very clearly marked on the front. Just in case any passengers have missed the point, the driver – who, now that you descry his features under his cap, looks very much like Jean-Claude Juncker – keeps calling out the stops ahead: common European taxation, a unified welfare system, an EU army.

Now here is the question. If you want to remain where you are, what should you do? Should you literally remain motionless, sitting rigid in your seat as the bus purrs along its route? Or should you politely disembark and wave it on its way?

We have already seen enough of the campaign to know that there is one song, above all, that the Remainers like to sing, namely anxiety about change. The EU might be remote, it might be self-serving, it might be frustrating and arrogant and expensive and wasteful and corrupt, but can we be absolutely sure that the alternative won't be even worse?

The implicit pessimism here, the low opinion of Britain and her capabilities, is staggering. There are 193 states represented at the United Nations (alongside the EU, which sits there as if it were a state). Of those 193, 165 are not members of the EU. And two of the three states which, on the UN's own metrics, are the best places to live, are geographically European nations that have a trade-based relationship with the EU instead of a political union: Norway and Switzerland.

Nowhere else in the world is there an assumption that political integration is a prerequisite for free trade and co-operation. Other countries take it for granted that they can live under their own laws while working with their neighbours and allies. New Zealand shows no interest in merging with Australia, even though that possibility was explicitly allowed for at the time of its foundation. Yet the Kiwis are not written off as insular Australosceptics who have failed to adjust to the modern world. Japan is not applying to join China. But people don't hector the Japanese for being nostalgic Sinosceptics who can't get over the loss of empire. Self-government is the normal condition for a modern democracy.

In any case, we shouldn't make the mistake of confusing the familiar and the certain. The status quo won't be on the ballot paper. What we face, rather, is a choice between two futures, both of which we can sketch with some confidence, if not with the total certainty to which some futurologists foolishly presume.

One future involves being part of the continuing political amalgamation of the EU, a process that has been rumbling along since 1956. The other involves a new relationship based on a common market, not a common government.

Look at the British referendum through the eyes of a Continental supporter of closer union. As we saw earlier, most Euro-federalists were not just content, but actively keen, to offer the UK a trade-based deal – what Guy Verhofstadt called 'associate membership', and Jacques Delors 'privileged partnership'. But Britain, in the event, did not secure such a status. Instead, because her prime minister was determined to rush through the referendum before the migration or euro crises got any worse, she secured essentially optical and declaratory changes.

Only in Britain did EU supporters make even a perfunctory, half-hearted effort to pretend that a new bargain had been struck. Other EU leaders smirked openly at a deal that was, in the words of Lithuania's leader (and former Eurocrat) Dalia Grybauskaitė 'a face-saving and face-lifting exercise'.[43] As the *Irish Times* put it, going into the final talks: 'The concessions sought by the UK are either marginal in substance or essentially smoke and mirrors. They do not, as Mr Cameron will no doubt assert, change the fundamental nature of the EU or its relationship with the UK.'[44]

The general opinion in Brussels is that the mountains heaved and brought forth a mouse. After years of grumbling, sulking and threatening, the British were presented with a take-it-or-leave-it offer to stay in on essentially unchanged terms. More than that, the other member states took the opportunity to spell out, in black and white, that there would be no further reforms – that Britain could not expect to get any further changes in future.

Now ask yourself this question. How will it look to Eurocrats if, after so derisory an offer, we vote to remain?

43 Twitter (@Grybauskaite_LT), 19 February 2016
44 *The Irish Times*, 19 February 2016

After years of yapping and snarling and slavering, the bulldog will have shown itself to be toothless.

Imagine what would happen the next time an integrationist proposal were to clank its way through the tubes and chambers of the legislative machine in Brussels – a proposal for the harmonization of social security, say, or for a common EU rate of corporation tax. I, as an MEP, would do what I usually do on these occasions: I'd say that the measure had no mandate in Britain, and that my constituents had never asked to belong to a European state. But now, my fellow MEPs would have an answer. 'Oh yes they did, Hannan. They just voted for precisely these terms. They just voted to accept the supremacy of the EU and its institutions. They just agreed to be part of our project.'

Never mind the risk involved in leaving. Ponder the risk involved in staying. The EU is going through as severe a bout of turbulence as any it has known. What it had regarded as its two greatest achievements, the euro and the Schengen Zone, turned out to be fair-weather schemes. Neither held up when the storms came.

EU leaders responded to the twin crises as they always do – by turning them into an argument for even more integration. And they have made clear, in the Five Presidents' Report and elsewhere, that such integration must apply to all twenty-eight EU states, not just to those that chose to abandon their frontier checks and their currencies.

A vote to stay in, in other words, is not a vote to hold our ground. It is a vote to acquiesce in what is coming. When the EU demands, whether by majority vote or by a judicial decision, that the United Kingdom join in more bailouts, or increase her budget contributions in line with other members so as to fund the new fiscal transfer mechanism, or accept a quota of non-EU migrants who have entered other member states illegally, we shall be in no position to say no – politically, legally or morally.

What, then, of a vote to leave? Is it, in that favourite 'Remain' propaganda phrase, 'a leap into the unknown'? Hardly. Britain would be voting to recover freedoms that she enjoyed, in most cases, up to the entry into force of the Maastricht Treaty in the 1990s. She would be voting to remain in the loose free-trade zone that covers the entire European landmass, while stepping back from the superstate. She would be voting, in short, to treat with her neighbours as an independent, self-governing country, like New Zealand or Japan. Leaving is, if anything, a leap into the known.

What would be the immediate consequences? Britain would reassert the primacy of her own laws on her own soil. She would retain or replicate EU rules only when there were economies of scale or other advantages in doing so. She would recover her seat at the global top tables, where these rules are often set. She would take back control of immigration policy, allowing her to decide who entered her territory and on what terms, and who might be removed. And, of course, she would make an immediate cash saving of £350 million a week.

Other than that, as Lord Rose says, the short-term effects will be slight. We should think of Brexit not as a radical break, but as a way to update our priorities in a changed world. The Eurocentrism of the mid-twentieth century is beginning to look not just atavistic but downright absurd. All the growth is happening on more distant continents. Britain, having so far stood aside from the euro and Schengen calamities, now has an opportunity to be part of that success story – to raise her eyes from the exhausted Old World and see the opportunities across the oceans.

All we need is the courage to act. We still sometimes think of ourselves, in the phrase that actress Emma Thompson recently used as an argument for staying in, as a 'tiny little island'. But in what sense are we tiny? Economics? Global reach? Population? Geography? Which does Ms Thompson imagine are the big, influential islands? Madagascar? Borneo?

Britain has the fifth-largest economy on the planet,

and is closing fast on Germany. She is ranked first in terms of soft power. Her brands, from Wimbledon to Manchester United, from the Duchess of Cambridge to *Downton Abbey*, are recognized around the world. Her language is the world's common medium. She is one of only five states capable of deploying conventional military force at distance. How much bigger must a country be before it can manage its own affairs?

Two futures beckon. Neither can be foreknown with total certainty. But there is one thing we know in our bones: a confident country does not fear to follow her own path.

EUROCRATS IN THEIR OWN WORDS

'From now on, monetary policy, usually an essential part of national sovereignty, will be decided by a truly European Institution.'

—WILLEM F. DUISENBURG
ECB president 1998–2003, 31 December 1998

'National sovereignty in foreign and security policy will soon prove itself to be a product of the imagination as none of the member states of the European Union has the potential or weight for a global role on its own.'

—GERHARD SCHRÖDER
German chancellor 1998–2005, 19 January 1999

'Our task is the creation of a new constitutional order for a new united Europe.'

—PETER HAIN
UK minister for Europe 2001–02, 21 March 2002

'If the answer is No, the vote will probably have to be done again, because it absolutely has to be a Yes.'

—JEAN-LUC DEHAENE
Belgian prime minister 1992–99, June 2004 (on a possible Belgian referendum on the EU Constitution)

'Yet there are those today who want to scrap the supranational idea. They want the European Union to go back to the old purely inter-governmental way of doing things. I say those people should come to Terezin [Nazi concentration camp] and see where that old road leads.'

—MARGOT WÄLLSTROM
Swedish minister of foreign affairs 2014– and EU Commissioner 1999–2010, 8 May 2005

'If it's a Yes we will say "on we go", and if it's a No we will say "we continue".'

—JEAN-CLAUDE JUNCKER
Luxembourg prime minister 1995–2013 and president of the European Commission 2014– , 25 May 2005 (on the French referendum on the European Constitution)

'The Constitution aimed to be clear, whereas this treaty
had to be unclear. It is a success.'

—KAREL DE GUCHT
Belgian minister of foreign affairs 2004–09
and EU Commissioner 2009–14, 23 June 2007

'The EU is a non-imperial Empire.'

—JOSÉ MANUEL BARROSO
Portuguese prime minister 2002–04 and president
of the European Commission 2004–14, 10 July 2007

'The euro has been a rock of stability, as illustrated
by the contrasting fortunes of Iceland and Ireland.'

—RICHARD CORBETT
MEP 1996–2009 and 2014– , 16 January 2009

'A Europe of nations is a relic of the past.'

—GUY VERHOFSTADT
Belgian prime minister 1999–2004 and leader of the
Alliance of Liberals and Democrats for Europe (ALDE)
Group in the European Parliament, February 2010

'The ultimate consequence of identity thinking is the
gas chambers of Auschwitz.'

—GUY VERHOFSTADT
Belgian prime minister 1999–2004 and leader of the ALDE
Group in the European Parliament, February 2010

'[Bailouts are] expressly forbidden in the treaties by the famous no-bailout clause. De facto, we have changed the treaty.'

—PIERRE LELLOUCHE
French minister for Europe 2009–10, 27 May 2010

'The time of the homogenous nation-state is over.'

—HERMAN VAN ROMPUY
Belgian prime minister 2008–09 and president of the European Council 2009–14, November 2010

'The European Union must take a decisive step towards a federal economic government.'

—ANDREW DUFF
MEP, September 2011

'The best way today to defend the interests of France and to defend the interests of Germany is to defend the interest of the European Union and to give more power to Europe.'

—GUY VERHOFSTADT
Belgian prime minister 1999–2004 and leader of the ALDE Group in the European Parliament, 28 September 2011

'Why is there such a problem in this crisis? Because member states are reluctant to transfer new sovereignty and powers to the European Union. And we all know that the only way out of this crisis is a new transfer of powers to the European Union and the European Institutions.'

—Guy Verhofstadt
Belgian prime minister 1999–2004 and leader of the ALDE Group in the European Parliament, 28 September 2011

'When it becomes serious you have to lie.'

—Jean-Claude Juncker
Luxembourg prime minister 1995–2013 and president of the European Commission 2014– , 20 April 2011

'Another suggestion that we can make to Her Majesty's Government is that, if it wants to make savings in the British public sector, it can do so by increasing the role of the European Union... If the British Government wants to make savings, it can join the euro, it can give the European Union more powers and responsibilities.'

—Guy Verhofstadt
Belgian prime minister 1999–2004 and leader of the ALDE Group in the European Parliament, 8 June 2011

'Without the European Union, this continent is a continent of disputes, war and even of genocide.'

—GUY VERHOFSTADT
Belgian prime minister 1999–2004 and leader of the ALDE Group in the European Parliament, 6 July 2011

'We must dare to take an even more radical leap: a leap towards a fully-fledged European nationality.'

—GUY VERHOFSTADT
leader of the ALDE Group, and Daniel Cohn-Bendit, former leader of the Greens/EFA Group, in their co-authored book For Europe!, *October 2012*

'A political union needs to be our political horizon.'

—JOSÉ MANUEL BARROSO
Portuguese prime minister 2002–04 and president of the European Commission 2004–14, 11 September 2013

'We need a political federation with the Commission as government.'

—VIVIANE REDING
EU Commissioner 1999–2014, 3 December 2013

'Europe is not the problem – Europe is the solution.'

—JOSEPH DAUL
MEP 1999–2014, 6 March 2014

'Our EU Treaties say that the euro is irreversible.'

—JEAN-CLAUDE JUNCKER
Luxembourg prime minister 1995–2013 and president of the
European Commission 2014– , 12 May 201

'It is time to recognize that this [European] Parliament is the real European Democracy of the European continent.'

—GUY VERHOFSTADT
Belgian prime minister 1999–2004 and leader of the ALDE
Group in the European Parliament, 2014

'If you don't want the strengthening of Europe, there is only one way. The only way possible for those who are not convinced of Europe, is to leave Europe.'

—FRANÇOIS HOLLANDE
French prime minister 2012– , 7 October 2015

'Such an army would also help us to form common foreign and security policies and allow Europe to take on responsibility in the world. One wouldn't have a European army to deploy it immediately. But a common European army would convey a clear message to Russia that we are serious about defending our European values.'

—JEAN-CLAUDE JUNCKER
Luxembourg prime minister 1995–2013 and president of the
European Commission 2014– , 8 March 2015

'These people call for insularity, less Europe, and a return to the nostalgic and misleading idea of the all-powerful nation state.'

—MARTIN SCHULZ
president of the European Parliament 2014– , 8 May 2015

'Britain belongs to the EU.'

—MARTIN SCHULZ
president of the European Parliament 2014– , 17 June 2015

'What is driving [the Commission] is not to be re-elected. That is why for us the political cost means nothing.'

—DIMITRIS AVRAMOPOULOS
EU Commissioner of migration and home affairs 2014– , 25 September 2015

LIES, DAMNED LIES AND STATISTICS

'I WISH SOMEONE WOULD set out the full, objective facts!' Yup, that'd be nice. In every election campaign, in every referendum, people ask, not unreasonably, for an impartial set of data, on the basis of which they can form their opinion.

The trouble is that there is no such thing as impartiality in politics. What one person considers objective, another regards as outrageously biased. It's how we're made: we all trust our hunches, pick the facts that sustain them and screen out the ones that don't.

If you can't find a single, neutral source, if everyone has prejudices and assumptions, then how are you supposed to get to the truth? By listening to the competing cases of the two sides. Referendums and elections work on the same basis as criminal trials. The two campaigns make their best case, like the prosecution and the defence, and then the voter, like the juror, comes to a balanced decision.

If neutrality is impossible, the best we can hope for is accuracy. This book, as you'll have gathered from the title, doesn't purport to be neutral; but I have tried to be accurate, in the sense of not using any false information or bogus statistics.

Several readers will disagree with my presentation of the facts. Pro-EU supporters often have a go at me, for example, for quoting our gross rather than our net contribution to the EU budget. I stand by my figures. After all, in every other field of politics, we quote gross rather than net figures. You can't imagine a parliamentary candidate saying: 'If you think about it, basic rate income tax isn't 20p in the pound, it's zero, because the entire sum is given back in roads, schools and hospitals.' Still, that's a legitimate argument to have. You might think I should quote the net figure; what you won't be able to argue, I hope, is that the gross figure that I give is wrong.

Let me turn to the claims made most frequently by the other side. The ten assertions below come from the glossy leaflet that was distributed to almost every household in Britain by the 'Remain' campaign group, Britain Stronger in Europe (BSE) campaign. As you'd expect, it makes some exaggerated and tendentious claims – this is, after all, a campaign, and that's what happens. But it also makes one or two assertions that cross the line into straightforward inaccuracy, and I think these are worth looking at, because there'll be a lot more of this before polling day.

Each of these claims is a direct quote from the BSE publication. I have chosen them because, in my experience, they are the ones that are most likely to keep coming up in debates.

'The benefits are worth £3,000 per year to the average household.'
Channel 4's *FactCheck* has called this figure 'fiction', and with good reason. It comes from a paper by the Brussels-funded CBI. The CBI didn't base its claim on any research; instead, it arbitrarily picked five estimates, evidently chosen because they gave pro-EU figures, and then plucked a figure from the top end of the range. As *FactCheck* says, the CBI number is 'way more optimistic than most other estimates, and we don't really know how CBI researchers have arrived at this figure'.

For most UK households, the three largest items are food, fuel and tax. All three ought to fall substantially outside the EU. Groceries will be cheaper because we will no longer have to subsidize Continental farmers. Fuel bills will fall without EU rules requiring us to buy more expensive alternative energy. And the £350 million we send to Brussels every week would be enough to give the entire country a 71 per cent council tax rebate.

'If we left the EU, the cost of imports [from the EU] would increase by £11 billion.'
This claim rests on the idiotic assumption that, outside the EU, Britain would impose tariffs on the other member states. But no one is suggesting that. Even Lord Rose, who heads the pro-EU campaign, has accepted that free trade would continue. As Lord Kerr of Kinlochard, our former Ambassador to Brussels, admits: 'There is no doubt that the UK could secure a free-trade agreement with the EU.'

A pan-European free trade area stretches from non-EU Iceland to non-EU Turkey, covering EU and non-EU states alike. Indeed, since the EU's association agreements in Moldova and Ukraine came into effect, the only geographically European countries that have chosen to stand aside are Russia and Belarus. A post-EU Britain would continue to trade with the EU in the way that, say, Switzerland does today. Indeed, Switzerland sells the EU four-and-a-half times as much per head from the outside as Britain does from the inside.

'Over 3 million UK jobs are linked to our trade with the EU.'
The dishonesty of this claim is staggering. It is based on the same false idea that Britain would stop trading with the EU if it were not a member. Why? No one argues that we have to form a political union with, say, Brazil or Russia in order to do business with those countries.

The economist from whose work the figure was taken, Dr Martin Weale, has said: 'In many years of academic research, I cannot recall such a wilful distortion of the facts.'

'Countries that want free access to Europe's market of 500 million have to accept free movement.'
Nonsense. To pluck a random example, the EU just signed free-trade agreements with Colombia and Peru.

No one suggested that free movement had to be part of the deal.

Outside the EU, Britain might want to keep a measure of labour mobility with other EU states. But we would recover the ability to decide whom to admit and in what numbers.

'Leaving would also mean our border controls move from Calais to Dover.'
The reciprocal stationing of UK and French customs officials on both sides of the Channel has nothing to do with the EU. It rests on two bilateral deals between London and Paris: the 1993 Sangatte Protocol and the 2003 Le Touquet Treaty.

'Being in the EU means lower prices in our shops.'
Au contraire, as we say in Brussels. Being in the EU means being inside the EU's Common External Tariff, and having to charge duties on imports from non-EU countries – especially on agricultural products, textiles and commodities, precisely the things that Britain sources from outside Europe.

Outside the EU, we would continue to have tariff-free access for EU goods, but we could extend the same deal to non-EU producers, not least the growing economies of the Commonwealth. As well as helping those countries, it would mean that the price of food, clothes and other goods would fall in Britain.

'We are an independent nation within the EU.'
Of all BSE's claims, this is perhaps the most shameless. The essence of the EU, the thing that distinguishes it from every other international association, is that its laws take precedence over the laws of its member nations. As Lord Hoffman, the senior judge, put it: 'The EU Treaty is the supreme law of this country, taking precedence over Acts of Parliament.'

BSE brazenly says that the idea that Eurocrats 'set our laws' is a 'myth'. In fact, on everything from what taxes we pay to what we can fish from the sea, from employment law to immigration, we must do as Brussels says.

'The UK gets £66 million of investment every day from EU countries.'
It's hard to see how BSE came up with this figure. According to the ONS, investment from other EU

states in 2014 was £5.3 billion, or £14.4 million per day – only 19 per cent of total inward investment in Britain, the vast bulk of which now comes from outside the EU.

Europhiles used to claim that investment would dry up if we kept the pound. They were wrong. Then they claimed that it would fall because calling a referendum had created uncertainty. In the event, we have had more inward investment since the referendum was announced than any country in the EU. According to Ernst and Young, 66 per cent of Asian investors and 72 per cent of American investors want Britain to have a looser relationship with the EU.

'Being in the EU costs each household less than a pound a day.'

The ONS says our gross contribution to the EU is over £50 million a day. That's enough to build and equip a brand-new NHS hospital every week. Enough to wipe out all the austerity savings in the last parliament twice over. BSE is deducting the money spent in this country from the total; but that assumes it is spent on things we would have chosen for ourselves.

'*We are safer thanks to the European Arrest Warrant.*'

Tell that to Andrew Symeou, a teenage Briton who was whisked away to Greece in what was very obviously a case of mistaken identity, and spent two years in that country – eleven months of them in prison – waiting for his trial. Or to the parents of my five-year-old constituent Ashya King, detained in Spain under the European Arrest Warrant because they had taken their child out of Southampton Hospital to seek treatment elsewhere.

EU supporters like to claim that the EU is about security, but Brussels rules make it harder for Britain to deport criminals. As the former head of Interpol, Ronald Noble, said recently, the dismantling of European borders has created 'effectively an international passport-free zone for terrorists to execute attacks on the Continent and make their escape'.

ABBREVIATIONS AND ACRONYMS

ALDE	Alliance of Liberals and Democrats for Europe
AMR	Advanced Market Research
ASEAN	Association of Southeast Asian Nations
BSE	Britain Stronger in Europe
CAP	Common Agricultural Policy
CBI	Confederation of British Industry
COMECE	Commission of Bishops' Conference of the European Community
ECB	European Central Bank
ECJ	European Court of Justice
EEA	European Economic Area
EEC	European Economic Community
EFTA	European Free Trade Association
EPP	European People's Party
EU	European Union
FCO	Foreign & Commonwealth Office
FTA	free trade agreement
GCC	Gulf Cooperation Council
GDP	gross domestic product

HMRC	Her Majesty's Revenue & Customs
IFS	Institute for Fiscal Studies
IMF	International Monetary Fund
MEP	Member of the European Parliament
Mercosur	Mercado Común del Sur (Common Market of the South)
NAFTA	North American Free Trade Agreement
NATO	North Atlantic Treaty Organization
NGO	non-governmental organization
NSPCC	National Society for the Prevention of Cruelty to Children
OBR	Office for Budgetary Responsibility
OECD	Organisation for Economic Co-operation and Development
OEEC	Organisation for European Economic Co-operation
ONS	Office for National Statistics
OPEC	Organization of the Petroleum Exporting Countries
PAYE	Pay As You Earn
REACH	Registration, Evaluation, Authorization and Restriction of Chemicals
RSPB	Royal Society for the Protection of Birds
SDLP	Social Democratic and Labour Party
TDI	turbocharged direct injection
TTIP	Transatlantic Trade and Investment Partnership
UNED	Universidad Nacional de Educación a Distancia (National University of Distance Education)
VAT	value-added tax
WWF	World Wide Fund for Nature
WTO	World Trade Organization

ACKNOWLEDGEMENTS

Several people amended and improved this draft, including Mark Reckless, Lee Rotherham, Oliver Lewis and Matt Ridley. Thanks to them. Thanks, too, to my agent Georgina Capel, who is as glamorous, elegant and metropolitan as any woman in Britain, but who has none-the-less been converted to the Leave side. Thanks to Nicolas Cheetham who, as well as being one hell of a publisher, has been my close friend for 30 years. And a special thank you to my wife Sara who, all the time that I have been away from home campaigning and writing this book in snatches, has been carrying our third child, due shortly after polling day.